✔ KT-558-181

THE HENLEY COLLEGE LIBRARY

Micha____ ___e

Office

2013

060584

THE HENLEY COLLEGE LIBRARY

In easy steps is an imprint of In Easy Steps Limited
16 Hamilton Terrace · Holly Walk · Leamington Spa
Warwickshire · United Kingdom · CV32 4LY
www.ineasysteps.com

Copyright © 2013 by In Easy Steps Limited. All rights reserved. No part
of this book may be reproduced or transmitted in any form or by any
means, electronic or mechanical, including photocopying, recording,
or by any information storage or retrieval system, without prior
written permission from the publisher.

Notice of Liability
Every effort has been made to ensure that this book contains accurate
and current information. However, In Easy Steps Limited and the
author shall not be liable for any loss or damage suffered by readers
as a result of any information contained herein.

Trademarks
Microsoft® and Windows® are registered trademarks of Microsoft
Corporation. All other trademarks are acknowledged as belonging to
their respective companies.

In Easy Steps Limited supports The Forest Stewardship Council (FSC),
the leading international forest certification organisation. All our titles
that are printed on Greenpeace approved FSC certified paper carry the
FSC logo.

MIX
Paper from
responsible sources
FSC® C020837

Printed and bound in the United Kingdom

ISBN 978-1-84078-572-2

Contents

4   Calculations   67

5   Manage Data   85

6   Presentations   107

7 Office Extras — 127

8 Email — 145

9 Time Management — 165

1 Introducing Office 2013

This chapter discusses the latest version of Microsoft Office, with its ribbon style of user interface. It identifies the range of editions, and outlines the requirements for installation. Also covered are the process of starting applications, features such as Preview and Save, used by all Office applications, Office document types and compatibility with the older versions of applications.

There's no upgrade pricing for retail Office 2013 editions, and they provide a license for use on one computer only, though you can transfer the license if you replace your machine.

Office 2013 applications are also available in the Office 365 editions on a subscription basis, and these have licenses for up to five computers.

See page 220 for more details of the options for Office 2013.

Microsoft Office 2013

Microsoft Office is a productivity suite of applications that share common features and approaches. There have been numerous versions, including Office 95, Office 97, Office 2000, Office XP (aka Office 2002), Office 2003, Office 2007 and Office 2010. The latest version, released in January 2013, is Microsoft Office 2013.

There are various editions, with particular combinations of applications. The Home and Student edition contains:

- Excel 2013   Spreadsheet and data manager
- PowerPoint 2013   Presentations and slide shows
- OneNote 2013   For taking and collating notes
- Word 2013   Text editor and word processor

There's a Windows RT (for mobile devices) version of the Home and Student edition, though the applications it provides have restricted feature sets.

The Home and Business edition of Office 2013 contains all of the applications in the Home and Student edition, plus:

- Outlook 2013   Electronic mail and diary

The Professional edition of Office 2013 contains all those found in Home and Business edition, plus two additional applications:

- Access 2013   Database manager
- Publisher 2013   Professional document creation

For business users there are two volume license editions. The Standard edition has all the applications from the Professional edition except for Access. The Professional Plus edition has all the products from the Professional edition with two additions:

- InfoPath 2013   Design and use electronic forms
- Lync 2013   Online messaging service

There are also several Home and Business editions of Office 365 which contain combinations of the Office 2013 applications made available on a subscription basis. These include the Home Premium edition and the University edition, both containing the same applications as the Office 2013 Professional edition, but with a preferential rate for the edition aimed at academic users.

Ribbon Technology

Whichever edition of Office 2013 or Office 365 that you have, the applications they provide will all feature the graphical user interface based on the Ribbon. This replaced the menus and toolbars that were the essence of previous versions of Office.

Hot tip

This result-oriented user interface was first introduced in Office 2007, and now appears in all the applications in Office 2013.

This shows the Ribbon in Word 2013, with the Home tab selected. This tab usually displays five groups associated with basic document creation – Clipboard, Font, Paragraph, Styles and Editing. Some additional contextual tabs appear when appropriate. Each group contains a set of related commands and icons.

The Ribbon contains command buttons and icons, organized in a set of tabs, each containing groups of commands associated with specific functions. The purpose is to make the relevant features more intuitive, and more readily available. This allows you to concentrate on the tasks you want to perform rather than the details of how you will carry out the activities.

Some tabs appear only when certain objects are selected. These are known as contextual tabs and provide functions that are specific to the selected object. For example, when you select an inserted image, the Picture Tools Format tab and its groups are displayed.

This shows the Picture Tools Format group which is added to the Home tab in Word 2013, when you select an inserted picture.

Microsoft Office 2013

For systems with touch-enabled monitors, Office 2013 offers a Touch mode ribbon with larger and more widely spaced icons (see page 14).

The Ribbon-based user interface also features extended ScreenTips that can contain images and links to more help, as well as text. The tips display as you move the mouse pointer over an option, and describe what the functions are or give keyboard shortcuts.

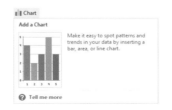

What's Needed

To use Microsoft Office 2013, you will need at least the following components in your computer:

Beware

These are the minimum requirements. A higher-speed processor, with additional memory and, for Windows 8 systems, a touch-enabled monitor, is the preferred configuration.

- 1 GHz processor (32-bit or 64-bit)

- 1 GB memory (32-bit) or 2 GB memory (64-bit)

- 3.0 GB available disk space

- 1024 × 576 or larger resolution monitor

- Windows (7 or 8) or Windows Server (2008/R2 or 2012)

Some functions will have additional requirements, for example:

- Touch-enabled monitor for controlling the system

- Internet connection for online help

- CD-ROM or DVD drive for install, backup and data storage

If your computer is running Windows 8 or RT, the system specifications will meet or exceed requirements for Office 2013.

Don't forget

These system properties are for the PCs used for this book, the Dell Inspiron 560 64-bit desktop (Windows 8 Pro and Office Professional Plus) and the Microsoft Surface RT 32-bit Tablet (Windows RT and Office 2013 RT). However, the tasks and topics covered will generally apply to any edition or operating environment.

Installing Office 2013

If you purchase a new copy of Office 2013, it will be downloaded onto your computer from where you can burn a DVD. Run the Setup program from this disc to begin the installation.

 1 Accept the license terms for Office 2013 when prompted

Don't forget

Select Customize to choose which particular applications you want to install, or to specify the 64-bit version of Office 2013. By default the 32-bit version is installed, even if there is a 64-bit operating system.

2 Select Install Now to accept the default settings and install all the Office 2013 applications in your edition

Hot tip

If you have an older version of Office, you may be offered the option to Upgrade the existing installation.

3 The applications are installed and Office 2013 is finalized

 4 Tiles for all your Office 2013 applications will be added to the Start screen

Start an Application

The first time you start an application after installing Office 2013, you'll be prompted to complete the installation settings.

Hot tip

This shows the Windows 8 Start screen. However, equivalent shortcuts are added to the Windows 7 Start menu.

1 Switch to the Start screen and select an application, e.g. Word

2 You'll be prompted to Activate Office

3 Enter your email address for a subscription to Office 365 and click Next

4 For a purchased Office 2013, click Enter a product key instead, type your license key and click Continue

12

Activate Office

To activate Office, enter the email address that's associated with your Office subscription.

Type your email address ✕

Next

Enter a product key instead

When you sign in, your documents and settings are online
Learn more | Privacy statement

Enter your product key

Your product key is 25 characters and is typically found in your product packaging.

See product key examples
Sign in with an active account instead

Continue

Don't forget

Setting up and activating the first application in Office sets up all the other applications in the suite at the same time.

5 Select Use recommended settings and click Accept then choose Office Open XML formats and click OK

First things first.

● Use recommended settings
Install important and recommended updates for Office, Windows and other Microsoft software and help improve Office.

○ Install updates only
Install important and recommended updates for Office, Windows and other Microsoft software.

○ Ask me later
Until you decide, your computer might be vulnerable to security threats.

The information sent to Microsoft is to help us and is not used to identify or contact you.
We take your privacy seriously.
Learn more

Accept

Welcome to Microsoft Office 2013

Default File Types ◻ Office

Microsoft Office supports many different file formats. Choose the format you would like to use as your default in Microsoft Word, Microsoft Excel, and Microsoft PowerPoint.

● **Office Open XML formats**
Choose this option to set your defaults to use the file format designed to support all the features of Microsoft Office.
Learn More

○ **OpenDocument formats**
Choose this option to set your defaults to use the ODF file formats designed to support the features of third-party productivity applications that also implement ODF. Many features of Microsoft Office are supported by ODF but some content or editability may be lost upon save.
Learn more about the level of support by ODF for Microsoft Office 2013 features

You can change this setting later in the Options for each application.

Learn more about differences between formats

OK

You can also add shortcuts for the Office applications to the Taskbar on the Desktop. To create the shortcuts:

 On the Start screen, right-click the tile for an application and select Pin to taskbar on the App bar that appears

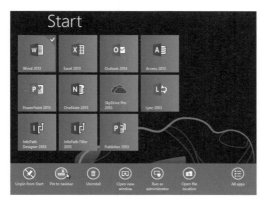

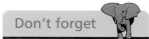

Don't forget

If you have Windows RT and Office RT on your computer, you'll find that the shortcuts for Word, Excel, PowerPoint and OneNote are already defined for the Taskbar.

2 Repeat to add any other applications that you want readily available

3 Press Escape to return to the Start screen and click the Desktop tile to see the revised Taskbar

Hot tip

The applications that are listed on the Apps screen depend on the edition of Office 2013 you have installed, e.g. there are 19 entries for Office 2013 Professional Plus, but only 7 for Office RT.

4 If any of your applications are not currently displayed on the Start screen, right-click the screen and select All apps

5 Right-click any application and select Pin to taskbar to add a shortcut (or Pin to Start to add a tile)

Application Start

Document-based Office applications open at the Start screen with the Recent Documents list and various Templates.

 1 Select an application tile such as Word or select the equivalent icon from the Taskbar to display the application Start screen

Hot tip

The Touch/Mouse Mode button appears by default when you have a touch-enabled monitor. To add it if not displayed, click the Customize Quick Access Toolbar button and then select Touch/Mouse Mode. You can then display the enlarged Ribbon on a standard monitor.

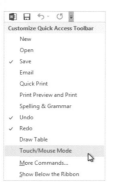

2 Select the blank document to begin a new editing session

3 Click the Touch/Mouse Mode button on the Quick Access Toolbar and select Touch

4 The expanded Ribbon is displayed

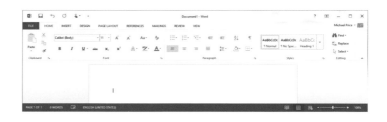

The Application Window

When you start an Office application such as Excel, PowerPoint or Word, the program window is displayed with a blank document named Book1, Presentation1, or Document1, respectively. Using Word as an example, the parts of the application window include:

BackStage (File tab)　Quick Access toolbar　Document name　Tabs

Help button
Ribbon Display options
Minimize/Restore/Close

Ribbon Command icons (display lists or galleries)

Collapse the Ribbon

Launch button (shows dialog box)

Vertical scroll bar

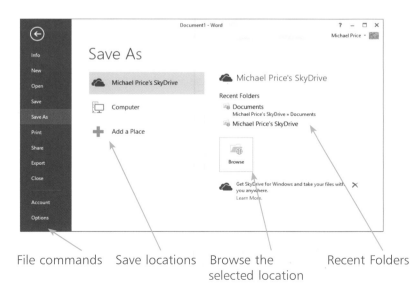

Status bar　Horizontal scroll bar　View buttons　Zoom level

When you have updated your document and want to save your progress so far, click File to display the BackStage and then select Save to name and save the document. You can save in your SkyDrive (see page 16) or on your computer.

File commands　Save locations　Browse the selected location　Recent Folders

Hot tip

The Save As dialog will open the first time you select Save for a new document.

Don't forget

From the BackStage you can select Info for details about your document, or New to start another document, or Open to display an existing document. There are also printing and sharing options provided.

Your SkyDrive

Hot tip

When you set up a Microsoft Account to sign on to Windows 8, or Windows RT you are assigned an allowance of up to 7 GB online storage which is managed on the Microsoft SkyDrive server (see also page 225).

To save your documents to your SkyDrive online storage:

1 Select File, Save As, choose your SkyDrive and click the Browse button

2 Confirm or amend the document name then choose the appropriate folder, e.g. Documents

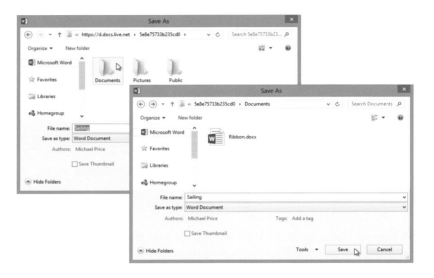

Don't forget

This means that you can access and edit the documents from any computer where you sign on with the same Microsoft account. You can also access your SkyDrive and documents from your browser.

3 Click Save to upload the document and save it in to your SkyDrive folder

4 To access your SkyDrive from your browser, go to web page **www.skydrive.com**, and sign in if prompted

If you are running Windows 8 (or Windows 7) you can download SkyDrive for Windows and keep a local copy so you can edit documents even when you are not connected to the Internet.

1 From File, Save As click the option to Learn More about SkyDrive for Windows

2 Select Download now, and click Run when prompted

3 The application is downloaded and installed, and the local SkyDrive is created

4 You find a link to the local SkyDrive under Favorites in File Explorer, and it is here that Office 2013 will now save documents when you select SkyDrive

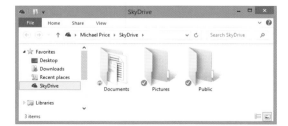

Don't forget

If you have Windows RT, this application is not available, and you cannot automatically sync a local copy of your SkyDrive.

17

Hot tip

You'll be offered the option to sync all your files and folders on the SkyDrive, or to choose folders to sync.

Live Preview

With the Ribbon interface, you can see the full effect on your document of format options such as fonts and styles, by simply pointing to the proposed change. For example, to see font formatting changes:

1 Highlight the text that you may wish to change, then select the Home tab

In previous versions, you would be shown a preview of the new font or style using a small amount of sample text. Office 2013 displays full previews.

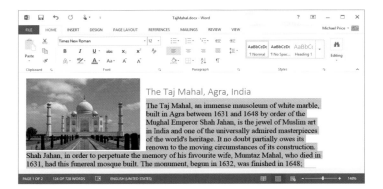

The Taj Mahal, Agra, India

The Taj Mahal, an immense mausoleum of white marble, built in Agra between 1631 and 1648 by order of the Mughal Emperor Shah Jahan, is the jewel of Muslim art in India and one of the universally admired masterpieces of the world's heritage. It no doubt partially owes its renown to the moving circumstances of its construction. Shah Jahan, in order to perpetuate the memory of his favourite wife, Mumtaz Mahal, who died in 1631, had this funereal mosque built. The monument, begun in 1632, was finished in 1648;

2 Click the arrow next to the Font box and move the mouse pointer over the fonts you'd like to preview

The selected text is temporarily altered to show the font (or the font size, color or highlight) you point to.

3 Click the font you want to apply the change to the text, or press Escape to finish viewing options

4 Similarly, preview the effects of Text Highlight Color or Font Color, Styles etc.

Working With the Ribbon

The Ribbon takes up a significant amount of the window space, especially when you have a lower-resolution display. To hide it:

1 Click the Collapse the Ribbon button (see page 15) or Right-click the tab bar and select Collapse the Ribbon

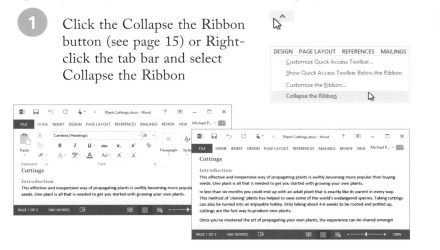

Hot tip

You can also select Ribbon Display Options on the Titlebar and choose Show Tabs to hide the Ribbon, or Show Tabs and Commands to reveal the Ribbon.

2 The Quick Access toolbar and the Tab bar will still be displayed while the Ribbon is minimized

3 The Ribbon reappears temporarily when you click one of the tabs, so you can select the required command

4 Alternatively, press and release the Alt key to display keyboard shortcuts for the tabs

Don't forget

Hold down the Alt key and press the keys in sequence, for a two-letter shortcut, such as Alt + FS (Font Size), and press Esc to go back up a level.

5 Press Alt + shortcut key, for example Alt + H to select Home and display the Ribbon and shortcuts for that tab

Quick Access Toolbar

The Quick Access toolbar contains a set of commands that are independent of the selected tab. There are five buttons initially:

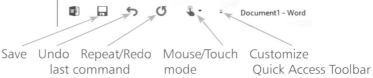

Save   Undo   Repeat/Redo   Mouse/Touch   Customize
last command   mode   Quick Access Toolbar

Hot tip

The Save As dialog will open the first time you press the Save button for a new document.

1   Click the Save button to write the current contents of the document to the SkyDrive or to the drive on your PC

2   Click Repeat to carry out the last action again, or click Undo to reverse the last action, and click again to reverse the previous actions in turn

Hot tip

You can right-click any command on the Ribbon and select Add to Quick Access Toolbar.

3   When you have pressed Undo, the Repeat button changes to become the Redo button which will re-apply in turn the actions that you have reversed

Add to Quick Access Toolbar

Customize Quick Access Toolbar...

Show Quick Access Toolbar Below the Ribbon

Customize the Ribbon...

Collapse the Ribbon

4   Click the Customize button to add or remove icons, using the shortlist of frequently-referenced commands

5   Click More Commands... to display the full list of commands, then add and remove entries as desired

Customize Quick Access Toolbar

New
Open
✓ Save
Email
Quick Print
Print Preview and Print
Spelling & Grammar
✓ Undo
✓ Redo
Draw Table
✓ Touch/Mouse Mode
More Commands...
Show Below the Ribbon

Don't forget

You can also click the File tab, then select the application Options and select Quick Access Toolbar to display this dialog box.

Word Options

General
Display
Proofing
Save
Language
Advanced
Customize Ribbon
Quick Access Toolbar
Add-Ins
Trust Center

Customize the Quick Access Toolbar.

Choose commands from:
Popular Commands

Customize Quick Access Toolbar:
For all documents (default)

<Separator>
Accept and Move to Next
Add a Hyperlink
Add a Table
Align Left
Bullets
Center
Change List Level
Choose a Text Box
Copy
Cut

Save
Undo
Redo
Touch/Mouse Mode

Add >>
<< Remove

Modify...

Show Quick Access Toolbar below the Ribbon

Customizations: Reset ▼

Import/Export ▼

OK   Cancel

Office Document Types

The objects you create using the Office applications will be office documents of various types, including:

- Formatted text and graphics   Word document
- Flyers and brochures   Publisher publication
- Spreadsheets and data lists   Excel worksheet
- Presentations and slide shows   PowerPoint presentation

Each item will be a separate file. By default, these will be saved in the Documents library for your username (logon ID).

1 To review your files, click File Explorer on the Desktop and select Libraries, Documents

Hot tip

The Documents library consists of the Documents folder for the current user, and the Public (shared) Documents folder.

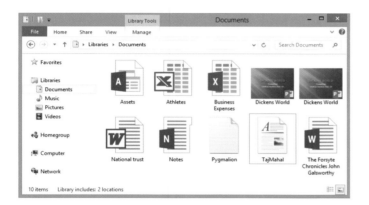

2 This shows files as large icons. For another style, click the View tab and select, for example, Details, to show the file information, including date modified, size, and type

Don't forget

You can specify another folder or subfolder for particular sets of documents, to organize the contents of your libraries.

Note that, in some applications, groups of related items will be stored together in a specially structured file. For example:

- Data tables, queries and reports   Access database
- Messages, contacts and tasks   Outlook folders
- Notes and reminders   OneNote folders

File Extensions

To see the file extensions that are associated with the various document types:

Don't forget

You can also change Folder Options in the Control Panel, under Appearance and Personalization.

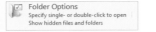

1 In File Explorer, select the View tab and in the Show/Hide section of the Ribbon click the box labelled File names extension

2 View the contents of your library folder

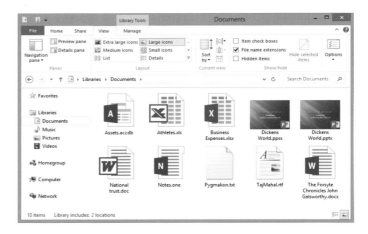

Don't forget

Files saved in Office 2013 use OpenXML formats and extensions, for example .docx and .xlsx. Older Office files will have file types such as .doc and .xls.

3 The file type will be shown, along with the file name, whichever folder view you choose

Compatibility Mode

Office 2013 will open documents created in previous versions of Office applications, for example .doc (Word) or .xls (Excel).

 Click the File tab and select Open, then click the down arrow for document type to list the types supported

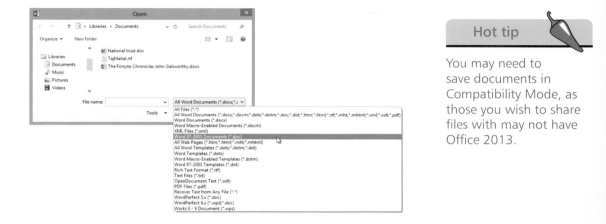

23

Hot tip

You may need to save documents in Compatibility Mode, as those you wish to share files with may not have Office 2013.

2 Choose the document type, Word 97–2003 for example, then select the specific name, e.g. National Trust.doc

Compatibility Mode

Don't forget

Compatibility Mode prevents the use of new or enhanced features, so the documents can continue to be used by systems with older versions of the applications.

3 Documents created in previous versions (including .docx files from Word 2010) are opened in Compatibility Mode

Convert to Office 2013

If you have opened a document in Compatibility Mode, you can convert it to the standard Office 2013 format.

1 Select the File tab and Info and click the Convert button

Hot tip

You can also click the File tab, select Save As, and choose the standard Office format (e.g. Word Document) to carry out the conversion.

2 Click OK to confirm, and the file type will be amended

Beware

Converting will create a file of the same name, but with the new Office 2013 format extension. The original file will be deleted.

3 To replace the original file, select File and then Save

Don't forget

With Save As, you have the option to change the file name, and the location for the new document.

4 To retain the original while creating a new file in Office 2013 format, select File, then Save As, and then click Save

2 Create Word Documents

This covers the basics of word processing, using the Word application in Office 2013. It covers entering, selecting and copying text, saving and autosaving, and proofing the text. It looks at the use of styles to structure the document, and at adding document features, such as pictures, columns, and word counts. It also discusses ways of creating tables, the use of Paste Special, and the facilities for printing.

Create a Word Document

There are several ways to create a Word document:

1 Right-click an empty space in a folder (e.g. Documents) and select New, Microsoft Word Document

Hot tip

The document will be named New Microsoft Word Document, though you can over-type this with a more relevant name. Double-click the file icon to open the document.

2 Start Word and select the Blank document (see page 14) to create a document temporarily named Document1

3 If Word is open, select the File tab, click New, and choose the Blank document to create another document to edit

Hot tip

The new document is given the next available temporary name, for example Document2.

Enter Text

1 Click on the page and type the text that you want. If the text is longer than a single line, Word automatically starts the new line for you

2 Press Enter when you need to insert a blank line or start a new paragraph

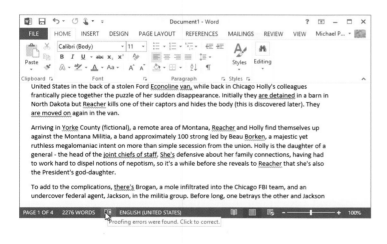

3 Proofing errors may be detected, as indicated by the wavy underscores – red (spelling) or blue (grammar and style)

4 Click the button on the status bar to correct them one by one, or correct them all at the same time, when you've finished typing the whole document (see page 31)

Hot tip

You can copy and paste text from other sources, such as web pages. Use Paste Options (see page 29) to avoid copying styles and formats along with the text.

Don't forget

You may see blue, wavy underscores to indicate contextual spelling errors (misused words), such as 'Their' in place of 'There'.

Select and Copy Text

It's necessary to select text for many purposes in Word, so it's not surprising that there are numerous ways to select just the amount of text you require, using the mouse or the keyboard, as preferred. To select the entire document, use one of these options:

1 Select the Home tab, click Select in the Editing group, and then click the Select All command

HOME
Find ▾
Replace
Select ▾
Select All
Select Objects
Select All Text With Similar Formatting (No Data)
Selection Pane...

2 Move the mouse pointer to the left of any text until it turns into a right–pointing arrow, then triple-click to select all the text in the document

Document1 - Word — □ ×
Prequels to Killing Floor
Although Killing Floor was the first book written in the Jack Reacher series, later books predate the events in that book. The Enemy is set eight years before, and The Affair is set just six months before Killing Floor. The short story James Penney's New Identity, features a pre-Killing Floor Jack Reacher.
PAGE 4 OF 5   93 OF 2372 WORDS   ENGLISH (UNITED STATES)   100%

3 Press the shortcut keys Ctrl + A to select all the text

There are many mouse and keyboard options for selecting a piece of text in the body of the document. For example:

1 Double-click anywhere in a word to select it

2 Hold down Ctrl and click anywhere in a sentence to select the whole sentence

Document1 - Word — □ ×
Prequels to Killing Floor
Although Killing Floor was the first book written in the Jack Reacher series, later books predate the events in that book. The Enemy is set eight years before, and The Affair is set just six months before Killing Floor. The short story James Penney's New Identity, features a pre-Killing Floor Jack Reacher.
PAGE 5 OF 5   18 OF 2372 WORDS   ENGLISH (UNITED STATES)   100%

3 To select a portion of text, click at the start, hold down the left mouse button and drag the pointer over the text, and release the button when the required text is selected

Hot tip

A single click selects just the line of text to the right of the arrow, a double click selects the whole paragraph.

Don't forget

Using the keyboard, you can press F8 to turn on Selection Mode, then press F8 once again to select the word nearest the insertion point, twice to select the sentence, three times for the paragraph, and four times for the document.

You can use text selection in combination with the Clipboard tools, to copy or move multiple pieces of text in the same operation. For example:

1 Select the first section of required text using the mouse to highlight it

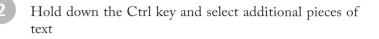

Don't forget

You can use the keyboard shortcuts Ctrl + C (copy), Ctrl + X (cut), and Ctrl + V (paste) instead of the Clipboard buttons.

2 Hold down the Ctrl key and select additional pieces of text

Hot tip

Click the Cut button if you want to move the text rather than copy it.

3 Select Home and click the Copy button in the Clipboard group

4 Click the position in the document where the text is required, then select Home and click the Paste button

Prequels to Killing Floor
The Enemy
The Affair
James Penney's New Identity
Deep Down
Second Son

Don't forget

Click the arrow below the Paste button to show Paste Options and choose between Keep Source Formatting, Merge Formatting, and Keep Text Only.

5 If you've copied several pieces of text, each piece appears on a separate line, so you will need to delete the end-of-line characters to join them up

Save the Document

When you are building a document, Word will periodically save a copy of the document, just in case a problem arises. This minimizes the amount of text you may need to re-enter. This feature is known as AutoRecover. To check the settings:

 Click the File tab, select the Word Options and click the Save command

By default, Word will save AutoRecover information every ten minutes, but you can change the frequency.

To make an immediate save of your document:

 Click the Save button on the Quick Access toolbar

The first time, you'll be prompted to confirm the location, the file name, and the document type that you want to use

 On subsequent saves, the document on the hard disk will be updated immediately, without further interaction

Beware

If the system terminates abnormally, any data entered since the last AutoRecover operation will be lost.

Don't forget

You can also select File, Save As, to specify a new location, name, or document type.

Correct Proofing Errors

When you've entered all the text, you can correct proofing errors.

1 Press Ctrl + Home to go to the start of the document, then select the Review tab and click Spelling & Grammar

2 For terms or proper names, select Ignore All or (if they are going to be used often) select Add to put them in your custom dictionary

3 For spelling errors, choose the correct word and then click Change (or Change All to correct all occurrences in the document)

4 Grammar and style errors are less definitive; you must decide about each suggestion on its merits and Ignore, Change or Revise as appropriate

Hot tip

The proofing (i.e. spelling and grammar) check will commence from the current location of the typing cursor, if you don't relocate to the start of the document.

Beware

Make sure that the appropriate spelling dictionary is enabled for the language of the document you are checking.

Don't forget

Each error is presented in turn (unless previous choices, such as Ignore All, cause the error to get cleared), until the spelling check is completed.

31

Change Proofing Settings

Don't forget

You can make changes to the settings for the spelling checks, and for the grammar and style checks.

1 Select the File tab, then Word Options and then Proofing

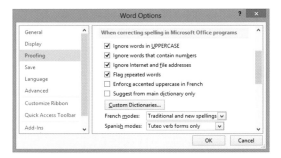

2 Some settings, such as Ignore words in uppercase and Flag repeated words, apply to all the Office applications

Hot tip

If you'd rather not use the grammar checker, clear the boxes for Mark grammar errors as you type and Check grammar with spelling. Alternatively, you can hide errors in that particular document.

3 Some proofing options are specific to the particular Office application, e.g. Word's Mark grammar errors as you type

4 Some options are specific to the document being worked on

Hot tip

The suggestions that are offered for these examples of contextual errors are:

seen →

see →

Where or Here →

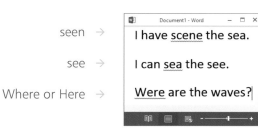

5 The spell checker in Word is contextual, identifying words that are spelled correctly but used inappropriately, and suggesting more suitable alternatives

Apply Styles

1 Select the Home tab then click in the main heading and select the style for Heading 1

**Don't forget**

You can change the style for parts of the text to suit the particular contents, using the Styles group on the Home tab.

2 Click inside one of the subsidiary headings and select the style for Heading 2

Hot tip

Click the down arrow to show the next row of styles.

33

3 Click within one of the text paragraphs and select style for No Spacing

**Don't forget**

Apply these two styles to other headings and paragraphs. To repeat a style, select an example, double-click the Format Painter icon, and then click each similar item in turn.

The spacing changes from the normal 1.5 lines to 1 line.

Outline View

When you have structured the document using headings, you can view it as an outline:

Hot tip

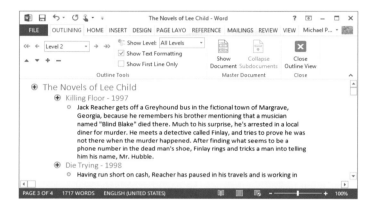

You can also click the Outline button on the status bar, to switch to the hierarchical view.

1 Select the View tab and click the Outline button, to switch to Outline view and enable the Outlining tab

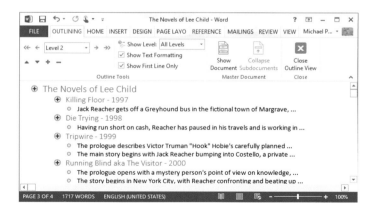

2 In the Outline Tools group, click the box labelled Show First Line Only, so that you can see more entries at once

Don't forget

Click the box Show Text Formatting to clear it. This displays the entries in plain text, to further increase the number of entries that can be shown.

This makes it easier for you to review the whole document. You might decide that you want to try a different sequence, for example chronological order of events rather than date of publication. Outline view makes it easy to reposition the entries.

1 Click the arrow next to Show Level, and choose Level 2

2 Locate an entry to move, e.g. The Enemy which precedes Killing Floor in date of action

Don't forget

This will display the selected level, and all the higher levels in the Outline of the document.

3 Click the Up arrow and the selected entry, with all its subsidiary levels and text, will move one row for each click on the arrow button

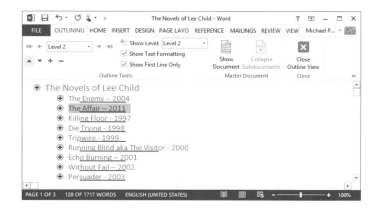

Don't forget

The Outline tools also provide buttons that allow you to promote or demote selected entries.

4 Repeat to reposition another entry, e.g. The Affair

Hot tip

You can click the + symbol next to an entry to select it, and then drag it to the required location.

5 Click the Down arrow to move an entry lower in the list

Insert a Picture

You can insert a variety of items into your document, including pictures, tables, headers and footers, WordArt, and symbols.

Hot tip

With Word 2013, you can also insert online pictures and video directly without having to download and save them on your computer.

1 Position the typing cursor at the location where the item is required, inserting a blank line if desired

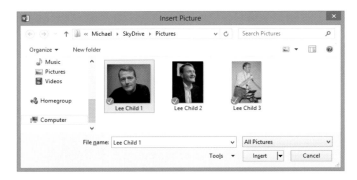

2 Select the Insert tab and click the appropriate icon or command, for example Picture (in the Illustrations group)

3 Locate the file for the picture, and click the Insert button

Don't forget

The picture will be added to the document, in line with the text. Note the addition of the Picture Tools Format tab.

You can adjust the position of the picture on the page of text.

1 Click the Position button in the Arrangements group and move the pointer over the buttons

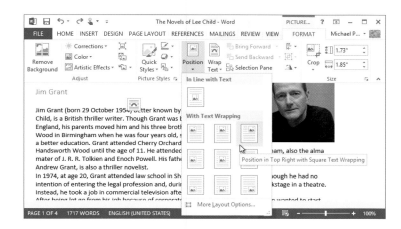

2 A live preview will be displayed. Click the appropriate button for the position you prefer

3 Click the up or down arrow on the height, to adjust the size of the picture. The width is changed proportionally

Don't forget

The Format tab allows you to change the size, select a frame, and adjust the brightness, contrast, and color of the picture.

Hot tip

Having chosen the layout, you can select the picture to drag the picture and make fine adjustments.

Don't forget

The original proportions of the picture will be maintained, when you make changes to the height or width.

Page Layout

The Page Layout tab allows you to control how the document contents are placed on the page, by just clicking one of the function command buttons in the Page Setup group.

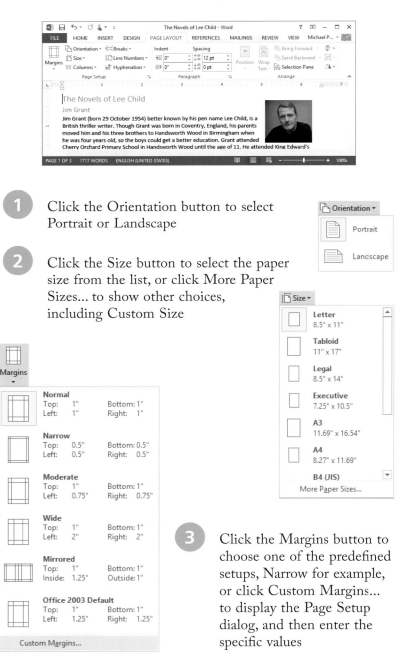

Hot tip

To display the vertical and horizontal rulers, as shown here, select the View tab and then click the Ruler box, from the Show group.

- ☑ Ruler
- ☐ Gridlines
- ☐ Navigation Pane

Show

1 Click the Orientation button to select Portrait or Landscape

2 Click the Size button to select the paper size from the list, or click More Paper Sizes... to show other choices, including Custom Size

Don't forget

You can also press the arrow on the Page Setup group bar to display the Page Setup dialog.

3 Click the Margins button to choose one of the predefined setups, Narrow for example, or click Custom Margins... to display the Page Setup dialog, and then enter the specific values

Display in Columns

1 Select the text you wish to put into columns and click the Page Layout tab then select Columns from Page Setup

Hot tip

Leave all of the text unselected if you wish to apply the columns to the whole document.

2 Choose the number of columns required

Hot tip

Choose Justify for the paragraph text, to help give the document the appearance of newspaper columns. Choose Center, for the title text to place it over the three columns.

3 Click in the body text, select the Home tab, click Select, Select Text with Similar Formatting, and click the Justify button

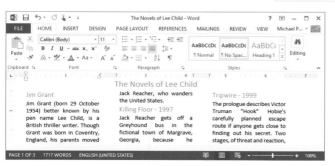

Don't forget

Select File, Options, Advanced, and choose to Keep track of formatting, to enable Select text with Similar Formatting.

Editing options
☑ Keep track of formatting
☐ Mark formatting inconsistencies

Word Count

If you are preparing a document for a publication, such as a club magazine, you may need to keep track of the number of words:

Don't forget

When there is text selected, the status bar shows word counts for the selection and the whole document.

97 OF 1717 WORDS

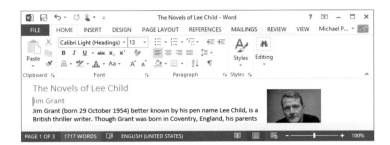

1 View the word count for the document on the status bar

2 Click the word count to display the detailed counts for pages, paragraphs, lines, and characters

Word Count	
Statistics:	
Pages	3
Words	1,717
Characters (no spaces)	8,170
Characters (with spaces)	9,856
Paragraphs	46
Lines	129
☑ Include textboxes, footnotes and endnotes	
	Close

Hot tip

You can also display the word count details by selecting the Review tab and clicking Word Count, in the Proofing group.

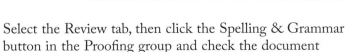

For a fuller analysis of the contents of the document:

1 Select File, Options, Proofing, then Show readability statistics

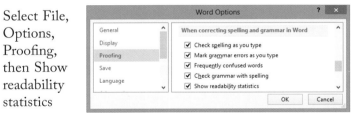

2 Select the Review tab, then click the Spelling & Grammar button in the Proofing group and check the document

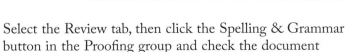

3 After the spelling check is completed, the document statistics are displayed

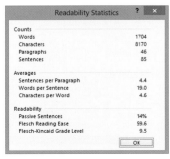

Readability Statistics

Counts	
Words	1704
Characters	8170
Paragraphs	46
Sentences	85
Averages	
Sentences per Paragraph	4.4
Words per Sentence	19.0
Characters per Word	4.6
Readability	
Passive Sentences	14%
Flesch Reading Ease	59.6
Flesch-Kincaid Grade Level	9.5

Create a Table

To specify a table in your document:

1 Click the point where you want the table, then click the Insert tab, and select Table

Hot tip

You'll see previews of the indicated table sizes as you move the pointer across the Insert Table area.

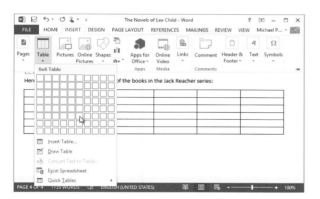

2 Move the pointer over the Insert Table area to select the number of rows and columns, then click to confirm

3 Type the contents, pressing Tab to move to the next cell

Don't forget

Press the arrow keys to navigate around the table. Click and drag a separator line to adjust the width of a column.

Convert Text to Table

Hot tip

Select Home, then click the Show/Hide button in the Paragraph group to display tabs and paragraph marks. Two consecutive commas or tabs indicate an empty cell. Paragraph marks separate the rows.

Don't forget

Select Autofit to contents, to adjust the column widths to match the data in those cells.

Don't forget

The cursor must be in the table area to display the Table Tools tab. Select Layout to apply operations, such as insert, delete, merge, and align.

If you already have the text that's needed for the table, perhaps taken from another document, you can convert the text into a table.

1 Make sure that the cell entries are separated by a comma or tab mark, or some other unique character

2 Highlight the text, select the Insert tab, and then click Table, Convert Text to Table

3 Specify your particular separation character and then click OK

4 The table will be created with the data inserted into the relevant cells, which may be expanded to hold the data

Lee Child Booklist
Here is a table showing some details of the books in the Jack Reacher series:

Number	Title	Published	Pages	IDBN-10	ISBN-13
01	Killing Floor	1997	522	0553816225	9780553816228
02	Die Trying	1998	374	0399143793	9780515142242
03	Tripwire	1999	343	0399144676	9780399144677
04	Running Blind	2000	384	0593043995	9780593043998
05	Echo Burning	2001	384	0399147268	9780399147265
06	Without Fail	2002	374	0425264424	9780425264423
07	Persuader	2003	352	0385336667	9780385336666
08	The Enemy	2004	400	0553815857	9780553815856
09	One Shot	2005	384	0385336683	9780385336680
10	The Hard Way	2006	384	0385336691	9780385336697
11	Bad Luck and Trouble	2007	384	0385340559	9780385340557
12	Nothing to Lose	2008	416	0385340567	9780385340564
13	Gone Tomorrow	2009	432	0385340575	9780385340571

Paste Special

To copy the text without including its formatting and graphics:

 1 Highlight the text you want, then right-click the selected area and click the Copy command

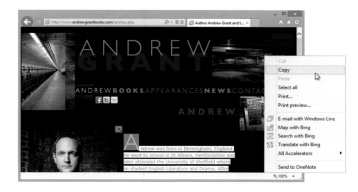

 2 Click in the document where the text is needed, and from the Home tab, click the arrow below the Paste button

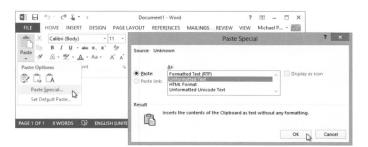

 3 Click Paste Special and choose Paste, Unformatted Text

Hot tip

When you copy information from other documents, or from web pages, the text may include graphics, formatting, and colors that are inappropriate for your document.

Beware

Graphical information won't be copied, even if it has the appearance of text (as with the initial A for Andrew in the text being copied for this example).

Don't forget

The copied text will inherit the format of that part of the document you clicked before carrying out the paste operation.

Print Document

1 To print your document from within Word, click the File tab and select Print (or press Ctrl + P)

Hot tip

In Office 2013 programs, you can preview and print your documents at one location – in the Print section of the BackStage.

Don't forget

You can view the document as it will appear in print by selecting the View tab and selecting the Print Layout button from the View group.

2 From here, you can preview the document, using the zoom slider, the scroll bars, and the page change buttons

3 Select the specific printer to use

4 Choose the pages you want to print, and adjust other settings, such as the paper size and the margins

5 Specify the number of copies, then click the Print button

Quick Print
You can add the Quick Print button to the Quick Access Toolbar (see page 14), to get an immediate print of the current document, using the default settings.

3 Complex Documents

Microsoft Word can be used to create and edit more complex documents, such as booklets and brochures. This chapter covers importing text, inserting illustrations, creating tables of contents, and illustrations. It shows how templates can be used to help create documents. It also introduces Publisher, the Office application that is specifically designed for desktop publishing.

Start a Booklet

To illustrate some of the facilities available for creating and organizing complex documents, we'll go through the process of importing and structuring the text for a booklet. Our example uses the text for *A Study in Scarlet* by Sir Arthur Conan Doyle.

Hot tip

The text for books that are in the public domain can be found on the Internet, at websites such as Project Gutenberg at **www.gutenberg.org**

1 Start by typing the book title, author, and chapter names

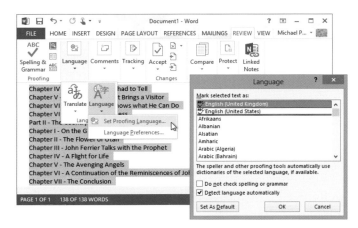

2 When you've entered all the chapter headings, set the language. This is a United Kingdom book, so press Ctrl + A to highlight text, select Review, Language, Set Proofing Language, English (United Kingdom) and click OK

Beware

You need to highlight all the text to change to a different language for the whole document.

Don't forget

By default, the first line of text will be used as the name for the Word document, in this case A Study in Scarlet.

3 Click Save on the Quick Access toolbar, and provide a name for the document, or accept the suggested name

Choose Page Arrangement

Now specify the paper size, the margins and the page style.

1   Select the Page Layout tab, and click Size to choose the paper size you are printing on, for example Letter

Hot tip

Similarly, you can click Margins to select the size you want to use, for example Normal.

2   Click the down arrow on the Page Setup group to display the Page Setup dialog

3   In the Pages section, select Multiple pages, Book fold

4   Specify the number of sheets per booklet

Don't forget

The orientation changes to landscape, and you get four pages of the document on each piece of paper (printed on both sides). A four-sheet booklet, for example, would be printed as:

Front

Back

You specify the number of sheets in multiples of 4 up to 40, to assemble the document in blocks of pages or choose All to assemble the document as a single booklet

Create the Structure

1 Highlight the text for the chapter titles

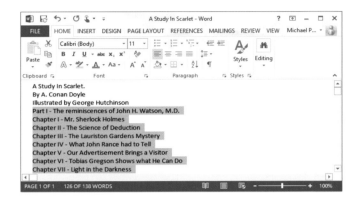

Hot tip

This particular book has two parts, with seven chapters in each part.

2 Click the Home tab and select Quick Styles, Heading 1

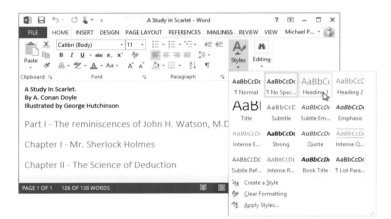

Don't forget

The formatting changes center the chapter titles over the text that will be inserted (see page 50).

3 With the chapter titles still selected, click the Center button in the Paragraph group

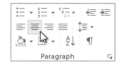

Hot tip

Steps 4 to 6 illustrate how you can use Find and Replace to insert special characters, such as line breaks.

4 To replace hyphens with line breaks in the chapter titles, click the Editing button and select Replace, again with the text for the chapter titles selected

5 In the Find what box, type a hyphen, with a space either side, that is " - " (without the quotation marks)

Hot tip

You can click the More button and select Special, Manual Line Break, to insert the required code.

6 In the Replace with box, type "^l" (the control code for a manual line break), then select Replace All

This changes all the occurrences in the selected text. Click No to skip the remainder of the document, to avoid changing hyphens elsewhere in the text

Don't forget

To see the paragraph and line-break codes, click the Show/Hide button (in the Paragraph group on the Home tab).

Note that each title remains a single item, even though spread over two lines.

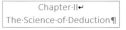

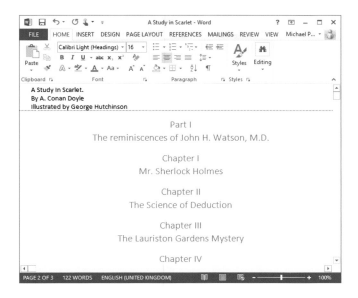

Import Text

1 Click just to the left of the Chapter I title, and select Insert, Page Break, to start the chapter on a new page

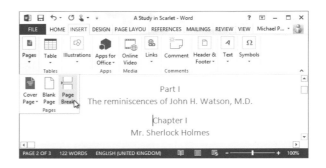

Hot tip

Type paragraphs of text, insert text from a file, or copy and paste text from a file, if you just want part of the contents.

2 Click the page, just past the end of the title, and press Enter to add a new blank line (in Body Text style)

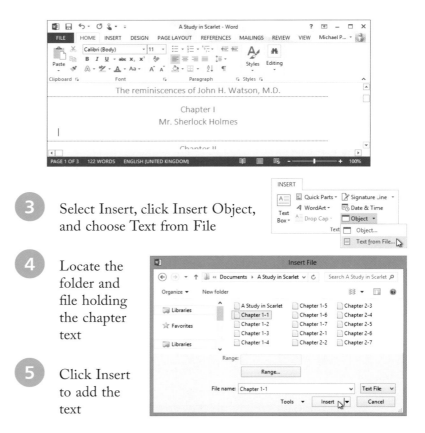

3 Select Insert, click Insert Object, and choose Text from File

Don't forget

This option was known as Insert File in previous versions of Word. It allows you to transfer the contents from various file types, including Word, web, and text.

4 Locate the folder and file holding the chapter text

5 Click Insert to add the text

6 Click OK to select the appropriate encoding, if prompted

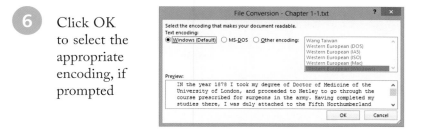

Hot tip

Step 5 is only required when the system needs your help in interpreting the imported text.

The text will be copied to the document at the required location.

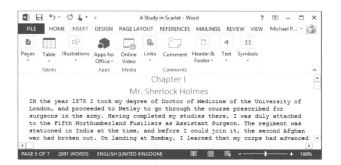

Repeat steps 1 to 5 for each chapter in the book.

To adjust the style for the inserted text:

1 Click anywhere in the new text, click the Home tab, then click Select and choose Select Text with Similar Formatting

Hot tip

The inserted text may not have the format you require, but you can change all the inserted text in a single operation to a style that you prefer.

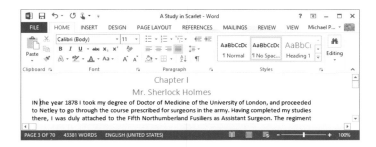

2 Select your preferred style, e.g. Normal, No Spacing, plus Justify and all of the inserted text will be converted

Insert Illustrations

1 Find the location for an illustration. For example, select Home, click Find, and enter a search term, such as Figure:

Hot tip

The sample text has the titles for the illustrations at the required locations, in the form of:
Figure: Title of illustration

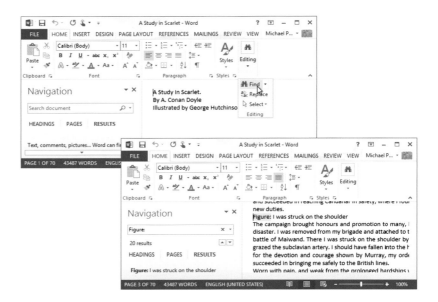

Don't forget

You can insert pictures from image files of all the usual types, including bitmap, JPEG (photos), and GIF (web graphics).

2 At the location, select the Insert tab and click Picture

3 Locate the file containing the required illustration and click Insert, and the picture is inserted into the document, in line with the text

4 Adjust its size and position as required

Add Captions

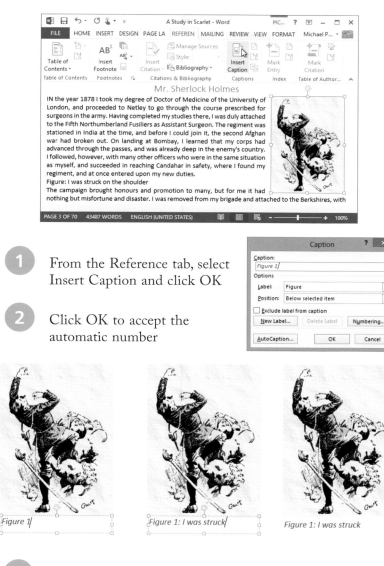

Don't forget

Repeat these two sets of steps to insert a picture and a caption for each of the figures in the book.

1 From the Reference tab, select Insert Caption and click OK

2 Click OK to accept the automatic number

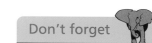

Don't forget

If the document doesn't already contain the title for the illustration, type it after the automatic number in the Caption box (or directly into the document after Figure #).

Figure 1/

Figure 1: I was struck/

Figure 1: I was struck

3 Type a colon and a space, then copy or type the text for the picture title to follow after the figure number

4 Click away from the caption to see the figure as it will appear in the final document

5 Repeat this procedure for each of the pictures in the document, until you have all the figures and captions

Hot tip

The captions that you create are used to create a table of illustrations (see page 56).

Table of Contents

When you have formatted text within the document with heading levels, you can use these to create and maintain a contents list.

 1 Select Home, Find, Go To, then select Page and type the number 2, then click Go To and Close, to show that page

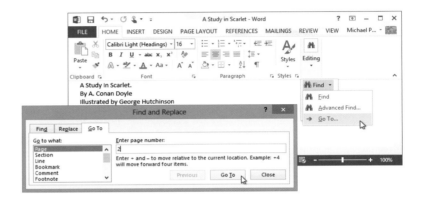

Hot tip

You can prefix the number with + or - to go forward or back for the specified number of pages.

54

2 Select the Insert tab and click Blank Page in the Pages group, to insert a blank page for the contents list

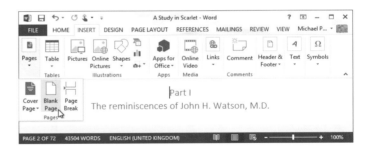

Don't forget

If the typing cursor is centered, select Home, and click Align Text Left in the paragraph group, before selecting the Table of Contents button.

3 Go to the new page 2, select the References tab, and click the Table of Contents button

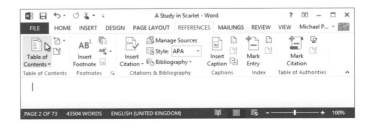

4 Choose the type of table that you want, for example Automatic Table 1 (with Contents as the title)

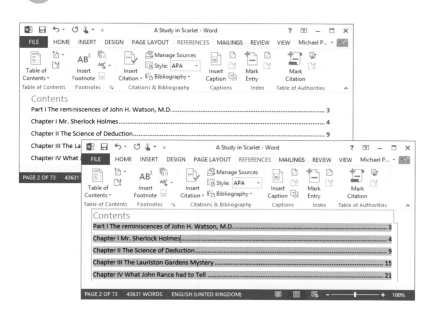

Hot tip

This type of table will use heading levels 1, 2 and 3 to generate the table. You can also build a table using custom styles, or based on manually selected text.

5 The table of contents is inserted into the document

Beware

The table of contents must be updated to show any changes to the heading-text content, or to the page-number value.

6 When you click in the table of contents, its entries are grayed, to indicate they are field codes (action items)

Don't forget

When you hover the mouse pointer over an entry in the table, with the shift key pressed, you'll have a link to the associated section of the document.

Table of Illustrations

 Go to the start of chapter 1 and insert another blank page, this time for a list of illustrations

 On the new page, type Illustrations, select the Home tab, the arrow to expand Style, and choose Heading 1

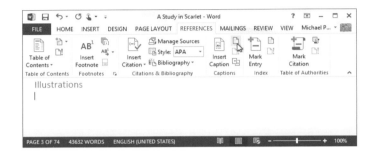

3 Press Enter to add a blank line, then, on the References tab, click the button for Table of Figures Dialog

4 Select the Caption label, i.e. Figures, then select or clear the boxes to Show page numbers, Right align page numbers and Include label and number

Don't forget

Entries for the chosen caption type, in this case Figures, will be identified and included in the table.

5 Click OK to insert the table of figures as shown in the Print Preview

6 The layout for the table of figures is similar to that of the table of contents created previously

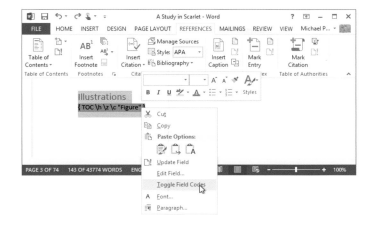

Don't forget

There's no heading included, so any heading required must be provided separately, in this case, Illustrations.

7 Click the table to see the grayed entries indicating that there are field codes and links to the figures

8 Highlight the whole table and select Toggle Field Codes

Don't forget

The format of the field code for the table of figures indicates that it is actually a TOC (table of contents) based on the Figure label.

Insert Preface

1 Go to page 2 (the contents page) and insert a blank page for the book preface

2 On the new page, type Preface, select the Home tab, the arrow to expand the Styles group, and Heading 2

Hot tip

If you want the preface to appear on an odd-numbered (right-hand) page, insert a second blank page in front of it.

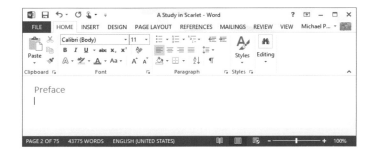

3 Press Enter and insert text from a file (see page 50), or type the text for the preface

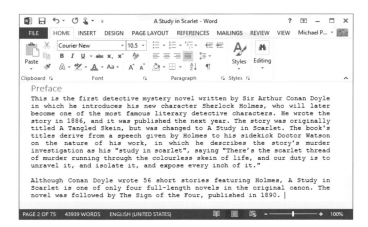

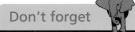

Don't forget

Save the document whenever you make substantial changes, to avoid the risk of losing your updates.

4 Adjust the formatting and alignment of the text, as desired, for example selecting Justify for the main portion

5 Select Save, on the Quick Access toolbar to save the latest changes that you have made

Update Table of Contents

When you make changes, such as to the preface or the illustrations list, that include new headings (level 1, 2 or 3), the table of contents is affected. However, the updates will not be displayed immediately. To apply the updates:

 1 Locate the table of contents and click anywhere within it

2 Select Update entire table to add new items to the table and click OK

3 New entries are inserted and the page numbers are updated as appropriate

PAGE 3 OF 75   43943 WORDS   ENGLISH (UNITED STATES)

Hot tip

Whenever you add text to the document, or insert pages, the page numbers for the entries in the table of contents change, but the changes will not appear until you explicitly select Update Table.

59

Don't forget

If you've added pages or text to your document, but have not changed the headings, select Update page numbers only.

Decorate the Page

Hot tip

Finally, you can enhance the formatting of the title page, using styles or WordArt.

1. Select a section of text, click Styles, and move the mouse over the options presented to preview the styles

2. Click your preferred style to apply that format to the selected text

3. For example, select the book title and choose the Title style. For other selections of text you can choose styles such as Subtitle or one of the various Emphasis options

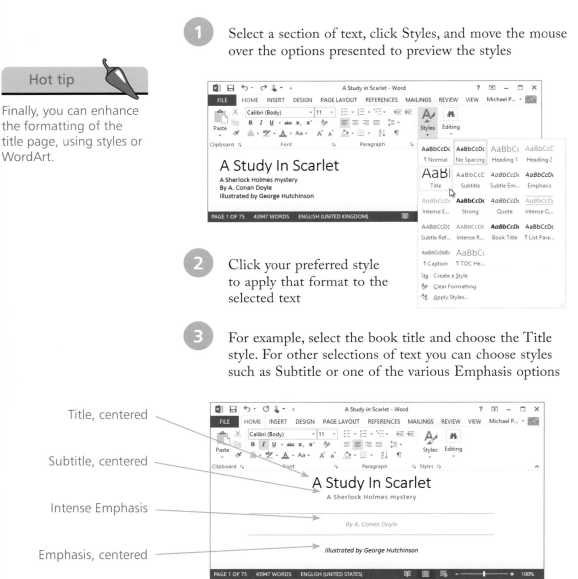

Title, centered

Subtitle, centered

Intense Emphasis

Emphasis, centered

4. Select Center if desired. Some styles, e.g. Intense Emphasis, are centered by default

5. For more impact select text and choose WordArt from the text group on the Insert tab

6 Review the WordArt styles offered and select an option

Hot tip

The WordArt effects are not displayed during Insert until you select a specific option. You can select a different option, or clear the WordArt if you change your mind.

7 The text is displayed in the selected style and color

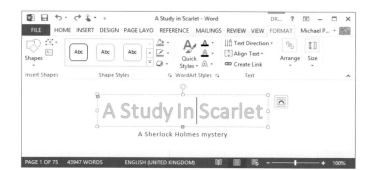

8 Explore the WordArt Styles, including Text Fill, Text Outline and Text Effects, and apply the options you prefer

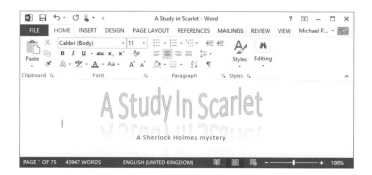

Don't forget

This illustrates the Full Reflection and Double Wave Transform, two of the options offered in the Text Effects.

Templates

1 Click the File tab, select New, and scroll through the featured templates to find one that meets your needs

Hot tip

When you need a specialized form of document, you can use a predefined template document to help you get started.

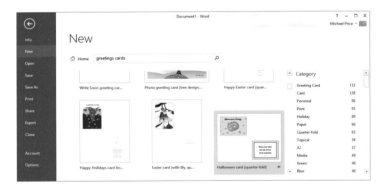

2 If there's nothing appropriate among the samples, search for online templates, using one of the suggested searches or providing a suitable search term, e.g. greetings cards

Hot tip

When you carry out a search, you will see a list of around 100 template categories, with counts of the number of templates in each category. Use this list to refine your searches.

3 Double-click the desired template, and click the Create button to begin the process of downloading the template and opening a new document based on that template

4 The template file is downloaded to your computer and saved on your hard disk

Downloading your template
Halloween card (quarter-fold)

Cancel

5 When the transfer completes, the new document based on the downloaded template will be opened

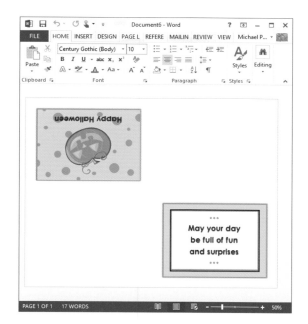

6 Change the contents of the text box to personalize the document, or delete the text for a handwritten message

7 Print the document, or Save it with an appropriate file name to work with it at a later time

Note that Templates in the older Word formats open documents in Compatibility Mode (see page 23). However, the document can be upgraded to the latest format when saved.

Microsoft Word

Your document will be upgraded to the newest file format.

While you'll get to use all the new features in Word, some minor layout changes are possible. If you prefer not to upgrade, press cancel and check the maintain compatibility checkbox.

☐ Do not ask me again

Tell Me More...   OK   Cancel

Hot tip

When you download a template, it is added to the list of featured templates, so it is easy to find if you need to access it in future.

Don't forget

This template is a four fold document and part of the content is inverted, so that it appears correctly when folded. Other templates may be two fold or single sheet.

Publisher

Publisher provides a higher level of desktop publishing capability, with a great variety of paper sizes and styles, including many templates for brochures and leaflets, etc., and lots of guidance.

Don't forget

Publisher is included in the Professional editions of Office 2013 and in all the Office 365 editions.

1 Start the Publisher application, which opens with the Start screen and a selection of document templates

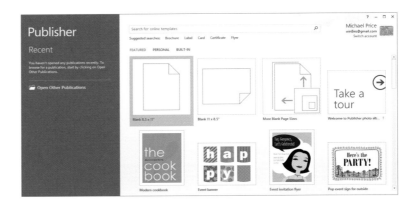

2 Explore the templates offered or search for online templates by topic, for example birthday

Don't forget

You can scroll through the images for a template with multiple pages. Click the [X] Close button to return to the list.

3 Review the selection provided, and select any template to see an enlarged version, and details of its format

Create a Publication

1 Choose a template, such as Party invitation and click the Create button

2 The template will be downloaded and a new document based on that template is opened

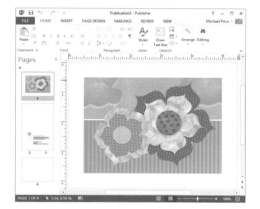

3 Click section 2 & 3 to see the middle portion of the card

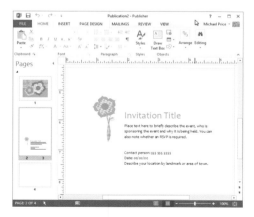

4 Enter the title and description for the invitation, along with contact and location details and save the document

Don't forget

The greeting card is divided into four sections, each one-quarter of the physical page, making it easier to view and edit individual parts of the card.

Page size: 5.5" x 4.25"
Paper size: 11" x 8.5"

Hot tip

Publisher offers various different sizes and layouts of greetings cards, for example:

1/2 A4 Side Fold 5.846 x 8.268" 1/2 A4 Top Fold 8.268 x 5.827" 1/2 Letter Side Fold 5.5 x 8.5"

1/2 Letter Top Fold 8.5 x 5.5" 1/4 A4 Side Fold 4.134 x 5.827" 1/4 A4 Side Fold 5.827 x 4.134"

1/4 A4 Top Fold 4.134 x 5.827" 1/4 A4 Top Fold 5.827 x 4.134" 1/4 Letter Side Fold 4.25 x 5.5"

1/4 Letter Side Fold 5.5 x 4.25" 1/4 Letter Top Fold 4.25 x 5.5" 1/4 Letter Top Fold 5.5 x 4.25"

Print the Publication

1 Select pages 2 and 4 to add the required text and images to those sections then save the final document

Don't forget

Note that Publisher shows the pages in a horizontal upright format, but will adjust the orientation of each page when you are ready to print the document.

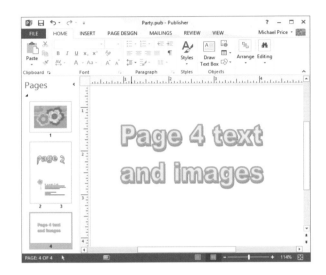

2 Select File, Print, to see the document as it appears on paper – a single sheet, with sections 2, 3 and 4 inverted

Don't forget

Once printed, the sheet is folded in half, and then folded in half again, to form the greeting card.

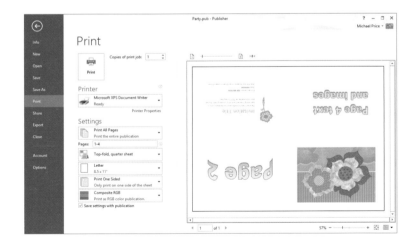

3 Adjust the settings as required, select the printer that you wish to use and then click the Print button

4 Calculations

This looks at Excel, the spreadsheet application, and covers creating a new workbook, entering data, replicating values, formatting numbers, adding formulas and functions, and using templates.

Start Excel

To start Microsoft Excel 2013 with a fresh new spreadsheet using the temporary name Book1:

1 From the Start screen select the Excel tile, or from the Desktop select the Excel icon

Don't forget

Alternatively, right-click an empty part of a folder window; select New, Microsoft Office Excel Worksheet.

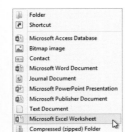

Double-click the file icon New Microsoft Office Excel Worksheet, to display and edit that document.

2 From the Excel Start screen select the Blank workbook to open an empty spreadsheet called Book1

3 You will find that Excel opens immediately with the blank document Book1, if you have previously selected File, Excel Options, General and cleared the box for Show Start screen when this application starts

The spreadsheet presented is an Excel workbook that contains, initially, a single worksheet which is blank. The cells that it contains are empty – all 17 million of them.

 1 To move to the last row (1048576) in the worksheet, press End, and then press the down arrow

Hot tip

There can be up to 1048576 rows and 16384 columns. This compares with 65536 rows and 256 columns in some earlier releases.

 2 To move to the last column (XFD) in the worksheet, press End, and then press the right arrow

If the worksheet contains data, the action taken depends on the initial location of the selected cell.

Beware

It may be impractical to utilize even a fraction of the total number of cells available, but the enlarged sheet size does give greater flexibility in designing spreadsheets. For larger amounts of data, you should use Access (see page 104).

3 If the selected cell contains data, pressing End and then an arrow key takes you to the edge of the data area

4 If the current cell is empty, you move to the start of the adjacent data area

5 If there's no more data in that direction, you'll move to the edge of the worksheet, as with an empty worksheet

	A	B	C
1		1000	
2		1010	
3	2000	1020	
4	2010	1030	
5	2020	1040	
6	2030	1050	
7	2040		
8	2050		
9	2060		
10	2070	3000	
11	2080	3010	
12	2090	3020	
13	2100	3030	
14		3040	
15		3050	
16			
17	4000	4010	4020

Don't forget

The movement is always in the direction of the arrow key that you select after pressing End.

Enter Data

Hot tip

You can find ready-made, budget spreadsheets and templates at the Microsoft Office website, and on other Internet locations. However, it is useful to create such a spreadsheet from scratch, to illustrate the processes involved.

The most common use of spreadsheets is for financial planning, for example to keep track of business and travel expenditure. To create a family budget:

1 Open a blank worksheet, select cell A1 and type the title for the spreadsheet, e.g. Family Budget

2 Press the Enter or down key to insert the text and move to cell A2, then type the next entry, Income

Don't forget

You can change the format of the labels to highlight entries, such as Title, Income, and Expenses (see page 76).

3 Repeat this process to add the remaining labels for the income and expense items you want to track, and labels for the totals and balance

If you omit an item, you can insert an additional worksheet row. For example, to include a second Salary income item:

 Click a cell (e.g. C4) in the row that's just below where the new entry is required, and select Cells, Insert, Insert Sheet Rows from the Cells group on the Home tab

Hot tip

Select a vertical group of cells to insert that many rows above the selected cells. Note that you can insert one or more columns in a similar manner, by selecting Insert, Insert Sheet Columns.

2 Enter the additional label, e.g. "Salary 2nd", in A4

Don't forget

You can also select the cell and press F2, or click anywhere on the formula bar, to make changes to the content of a cell.

	A	B
2	Income	
3	Salary 1st	
4	Salary 2nd	

3 Double-click an existing cell to edit or retype the entry, to change "Salary" to "Salary 1st" in A3 for example

71

Quick Fill

You can create one column of data, then let Excel replicate the cell contents for you. For example:

1 Enter month and values in column C, January in C2 and values in cells C3–C7 and C10–C15, for example

Don't forget

You can widen column A to accommodate the whole text (see page 78), then delete column B.

Hot tip

Click in cell C2, hold down the Shift key and click in cell C15 to highlight the whole range of cells.

2 Highlight cells C2–C15, move the mouse pointer over the box at the bottom right, and, when it becomes a **+,** drag it to the right to replicate the cells for further months

3 Release the mouse pointer when the required number of columns is indicated

Hot tip

Excel detects weekdays to create a series, such as Monday, Tuesday...; and it detects abbreviated names, such as Jan, Feb... or Mon, Tue... and so on.

Don't forget

Having initialized the cells, you can edit or replace the contents of individual cells to finalize the data.

4 Numeric values are duplicated, but the month name is detected and the succeeding months are inserted

After you've used the Fill handle, the Auto Fill Options button appears. Click this to control the action, for example to replicate the formatting only, or to copy cells without devising a series such as Months.

5 As you enter data into the worksheet, remember to periodically click the Save button on the Quick Access toolbar

Don't forget

The first time you click the Save button, you'll be prompted to provide a file name in place of the default Book1.

Sums and Differences

When you've entered the data, and made the changes required, you can introduce functions and formulas to complete the worksheet.

1 Click cell C8 (total income for January), then select the Home tab and click Editing and then AutoSum to sum the adjacent values

Don't forget

The numerical cells in a block immediately adjacent to the selected cell will be selected, and included in the AutoSum function. Always check that Excel has selected the appropriate cells.

2 Press Enter to show the total, then repeat the procedure for cell C16 (total expenses for January)

3 Click in cell C17 (the cell reserved for the net balance for the month of January)

4 Type =, click C8, type -, and then click C16 (to calculate total income for January minus total expenses for January)

Hot tip

The = symbol indicates that the following text is a formula. You can type the cell references, or click on the cell itself, and Excel will enter the appropriate reference.

5 Press Enter to complete the formula and display the result

6 Select cell C8 and use the Fill handle to replicate the formula for the other months (e.g. February to June), and repeat this process for cells C16 and C17

Don't forget

When the formula is replicated, the cell references, e.g. C8:C16, are incremented, to D8:D16, E8:E16 etc.

Formatting

Hot tip

Changing the format for various parts of the worksheet can make it easier to review and assess the results.

Don't forget

You can change each cell individually, or press Ctrl and click each of the cells to select them, then apply the changes to all the cells at once.

1 Click A1 (the title cell), then select the Home tab, choose a larger font size, and select a font effect, such as Bold

2 Press Shift, and click H1 to highlight the row across the data, then click the Merge and Center button

3 Click the Categories and Totals labels (e.g. A2, A8, A9, A16, A17), and change the font size and effects

4 Alternatively, click Cell Styles to pick a suitable style for the selection

To emphasize the "Net Balance" values for each month:

1 Select the range of cells, e.g. C17:H17

Hot tip

Excel 2013 includes a very useful Conditional Formatting facility, where the effects applied depend on the actual contents of the cells being formatted.

2 Select Styles, Conditional Formatting, Color Scales and choose for example the Green–Yellow–Red color scale

3 The cells are colored and shaded appropriately for the values that they contain

Don't forget

Positive balances are green; the larger the balance, the deeper the shade. Modest balances are yellow; while shades of red are applied to negative balances.

Rounding Up

You can use Excel functions, such as Round Up or Ceiling, to adjust the solutions of numerical problems, such as the number of tiles needed to cover the floor area of a room.

1 Open a new, blank worksheet, and enter these labels in the first column:

Number of Tiles
Tile Length
Tile Width
Room Length
Room Width
Number of Tiles
Per Box
Boxes

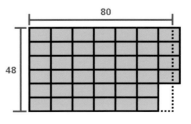

Hot tip

Double-click the separator bar between the A and B headings to adjust the width, to contain the longest entry.

2 Enter sample sizes in cells B2:B5, making sure that you use the same units for the tile and room dimensions

3 In cell B6, type the formula =(B4/B2)*(B5/B3)

Don't forget

The number of tiles in cell B6 is the calculated quantity of tiles required to cover the floor space exactly.

4 In cell B8, type the formula =B6/B7

For these figures, and on the basis of these calculations, you might think 5 boxes would be sufficient. However, if you fit the tiles to the area, you find that some tiles have to be trimmed. The wastage leaves part of the area uncovered.

Beware

You need to calculate whole numbers of tiles, allowing for wastage where tiles need to be cut to fit.

To ensure that there are enough whole tiles to completely cover the area, you need to round up the evaluations:

 1 Copy B2:B8 to C2:C8, and, in cell C6, type the formula =CEILING(B4/B2,1)*CEILING(B5/B3,1)

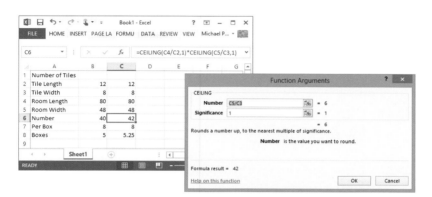

Hot tip

The CEILING function rounds the results up to the next significant value, in this case, the next highest integer. If the tiles have a repeat pattern, you might need to use the pattern size as the significant number.

The number of whole tiles increases to 42, which will now cover the complete floor area, even after cutting.

This gives 5.25 boxes. Assuming that boxes must be purchased in whole numbers, this result also needs rounding up.

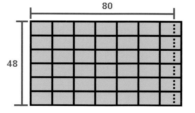

79

Don't forget

The ROUNDUP function is another way to adjust values. Here it is used to round up the result to zero decimal places, which also gives the next highest integer.

2 Copy C2:C8 to D2:D8, and, in cell D8, type the formula =ROUNDUP(D6/D7,0) to get the result: 6 boxes

Find a Function

There are a large number of functions available in Excel, they are organized into a library of groups to make it easier to find the one you need.

Hot tip

Clicking the More Functions button will display a secondary list of categories.

Don't forget

You can also click the Insert Function button on the formula bar.

Hot tip

Enter keywords related to the activity you want to perform, and Excel will list all potentially relevant functions.

Don't forget

The function arguments for the selected function are shown, and a brief description is provided.

1 Select the Formulas tab to show the Function Library

2 Click a category in the Function Library, for an alphabetic list of functions it offers

3 If you don't know where to search for the function you want, click the Insert Function button

4 Choose a category, e.g. Financial, and pick a function from the list offered

5 Alternatively, type a description and click Go, then select one of the recommended functions

6 Select a suitable function, e.g. PMT, and click OK

Don't forget

Rate is the interest rate for the payment interval (e.g. per month), Nper is the number of periods (e.g. number of months), and Pv is the present value (loan amount).

7 Type the values for the arguments (Rate, Nper, etc.), using the description provided as you select each item

Hot tip

You can, optionally, provide a final value, Fv (the cash balance), and also specify the Type (payments made at the start or the end of each period).

8 The result is displayed (a negative figure, indicating a payment) and the function is inserted into the worksheet

Goal Seeking

Using the PMT function, you can establish the monthly payments required to pay off a long-term loan over, say, 25 years.

Hot tip

To calculate payments for an interest-only loan, set Fv (see page 81) to the same value as the loan amount.

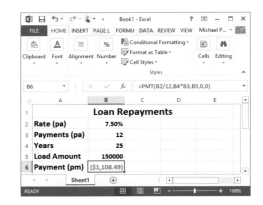

Suppose, however, you'd like to know how many years it will take to pay off the loan if you increase the payments to, say, $1500.

1 One way to establish this is by trial and error, adjusting the number of years until you get the required payment

Don't forget

You would carry on refining your estimate, e.g. trying 12 then 14, to discover that the correct answer lies between these two periods.

2 Try 20 years, then 15 years, then 10 years, the payment then goes above $1500. So the appropriate period would be between 10 and 15 years

However, Excel provides an automatic way to apply this type of process, and this can give you an exact answer very quickly.

1 Click the cell containing the function, select the Data tab, and click the What If Analysis button in Data Tools

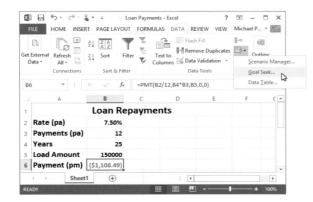

Hot tip

Use the Scenario Manager to create a set of results for a range of values, such as 10, 15 and 20 years of repayments.

2 Select the Goal Seek option and specify the required result -1500 (the payment per month) and the change to cell B4 (the number of years for full repayment)

3 Goal Seeking tries out various values for the changing cell, until the desired solution is found

Beware

You must specify the target payment as a negative value, since it is a repayment, otherwise Goal Seeking will be unable to find a solution.

4 Click OK to see the revised results displayed in the worksheet

83

Templates

Hot tip

You can get started with your worksheet by using one of the ready-made templates, which are offered for many common requirements.

1 Select the File tab and click the New button

2 Select any of the featured templates to view its content, and click Create to open a document using the template

3 Alternatively, select a category to review the templates from Microsoft Office Online

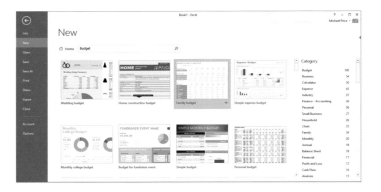

Don't forget

Check periodically to find out what new templates have been added to the Office Online website.

4 Choose a template to see the layout, and click Create to download your preferred template and open a document using that template

5 Manage Data

Excel also manages data, so we will look at importing data, applying sorts and filters, and selecting specific sets of data. The data can be used to create a chart, or you can arrange the data in tables, insert totals and computations, and look up values. Some editions of Office include Access, which offers full database management functions.

Import Data

You don't always need to type in all the information in your worksheets, if the data is already available in another application. For example, to import data from a delimited text file:

Hot tip

Excel can retrieve data from any application that can create files in a delimited text file format, such as CSV (comma-separated values), or from database systems, such as SQL Server, Access, dBase, FoxPro, Oracle, and Paradox.

1 Click the File tab and select Open

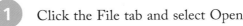

Don't forget

Identify the appropriate file type to select from, in this case, Text Files.

2 Select the file that contains the data you wish to import and click Open to start the Text Import Wizard, which recognizes the delimited file. Click Next to continue

Hot tip

Select My data has headers if appropriate, so that the header line is treated separately.

3 Choose the delimiter (e.g. Comma) and click Next

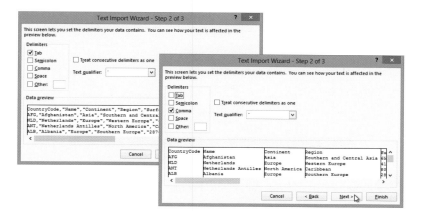

Hot tip

When you choose a delimiter, you can see the effect on the text in the preview area.

4 Adjust column formats, if required, then click Finish

Don't forget

The default format is General, which will handle most situations, but you can select specific data formats where appropriate.

5 The data is presented in the form of an Excel worksheet

Explore the Data

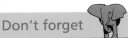

Don't forget

Select the File tab, click Save As and choose file type Excel Workbook, to save the data as a standard Excel file.

1 Double-click or drag the separators between the columns to reveal more of the data they contain

2 Select the View tab, click Freeze Panes in the Window group, and select Freeze Top Row

Hot tip

Freezing the top row makes the headings it contains visible, whichever part of the worksheet is being displayed.

3 Press Ctrl + End to move to the last cell in the data area and again adjust column widths as desired

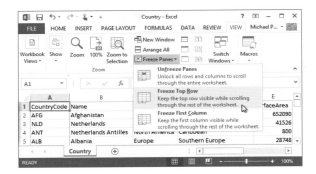

Hot tip

This will show you how many rows and columns there are in the data (in this example, 240 rows and 14 columns).

Sort

1 Click a cell in the Name column, select the Data tab and click the A–Z (ascending) button to sort by name

	A	B			E	F	G
1	CountryCode	Name			SurfaceArea	IndepYear	Population
2	AFG	Afghanistan	Asia	Southern and Central Asia	652090	1919	22720000
3	ALB	Albania	Europe	Southern Europe	28748	1912	3401200
4	DZA	Algeria	Africa	Northern Africa	2381741	1962	31471000
5	ASM	American Samoa	Oceania	Polynesia	199		68000
6	AND	Andorra	Europe	Southern Europe	468	1278	78000

Don't forget

You can also select the Sort options from within the Editing group on the Home tab.

Σ AutoSum ·
↓ Fill ·
← Clear ·   Sort & Find &
              Filter · Select ·

↑ Sort Smallest to Largest
↓ Sort Largest to Smallest
↕ Custom Sort...
▽ Filter
⊽ Clear
⊽ Reapply

2 Click a cell in the Population column and click the Z–A (sort descending) button, to sort from highest to lowest

	A	B	C	D	E	F	G
1	CountryCode	Name	Continent	Region	SurfaceArea	IndepYear	Population
2	CHN	China	Asia	Eastern Asia	9572900	-1523	1277558000
3	IND	India	Asia	Southern and Central Asia	3287263	1947	1013662000
4	USA	United States	North America	North America	9363520	1776	278357000
5	IDN	Indonesia	Asia	Southeast Asia	1904569	1945	212107000
6	BRA	Brazil	South America	South America	8547403	1822	170115000

Hot tip

If you click in a single cell, Excel will select all the surrounding data and sort the rows of contiguous data into the required order.

3 To sort by more than one value, click the Sort button

Sort

Add Level | Delete Level | Copy Level | ▲ ▼ | Options... | ☑ My data has headers

Column		Sort On		Order	
Sort by	Population	Values		Largest to Smallest	

OK | Cancel

Don't forget

You can sort the data into sequence using several levels of values.

...cont'd

Beware

If a selection of the worksheet is highlighted when you click one of the buttons, the sort may be restricted to the selected data.

④ Click the arrow in the Sort by box and select the main sort value, for example, Continent

⑤ Click the Add Level button and select the additional sort values, for example, Region and then Population

Don't forget

For data organized by columns, rather than rows, click the Options button and select Sort left to right.

⑥ Change the sort sequence, if needed, then click OK to sort the data by population within region and continent

	A	B	C	D	E	F	G
1	CountryCode	Name	Continent	Region	SurfaceArea	IndepYear	Population
194	USA	United States	North America	North America	9363520	1776	278357000
195	CAN	Canada	North America	North America	9970610	1867	31147000
196	BMU	Bermuda	North America	North America	53		65000
197	GRL	Greenland	North America	North America	2166090		56000
198	SPM	Saint Pierre and I	North America	North America	242		7000
199	AUS	Australia	Oceania	Australia and New Zealand	7741220	1901	18886000
200	NZL	New Zealand	Oceania	Australia and New Zealand	270534	1907	3862000
201	CXR	Christmas Island	Oceania	Australia and New Zealand	135		2500
202	NFK	Norfolk Island	Oceania	Australia and New Zealand	36		2000

Filters

You can filter the data to hide entries that are not of immediate interest.

 1 Click a cell within the data area, select the Data tab and click the Filter button in the Sort & Filter group

You can also select the Filter button from within the Editing group on the Home tab (see page 89).

2 Click a filter icon, e.g. Continent, to display its AutoFilter

Filtering is turned on, and a filter icon (an arrow) is added to each heading, with an initial setting of Showing All.

3 Click the Select All box, to deselect all entries, then select the specific entry you want, e.g. Oceania

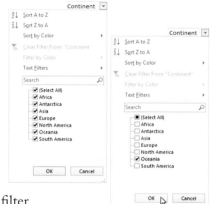

4 Click OK to apply the filter

Number Filters

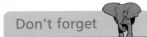

Don't forget

You can set number filters, where you specify a level at which to accept or reject entries, or choose an option, such as accepting the top 10 entries.

1 Display the AutoFilter for Population and choose all entries greater than 100,000

2 The filter icons for modified AutoFilters are changed, to show that filtering is in effect for those particular columns

3 Click a filter icon and select the Clear Filter option, to remove the filter for a particular column

4 The filter icon for that column reverts to an arrow, and the Showing All option will be applied

Beware

If you click the Filter button on the Data tab, or the Home tab, it will remove all the filters and delete all the filter settings.

Select Specific Data

Suppose you want to examine the population values for the larger countries. You can hide away information that's not relevant for that purpose:

1 Use the AutoFilter on the Population column, to display only countries whose populations are greater than 150 million

Hot tip

Filter the rows and hide selected columns to remove the data not needed at the moment from view.

2 Click column A, press Ctrl, click columns C, D etc. and select Home, Format, Hide & Unhide, Hide Columns

3 The display will be restricted to specific data, which you can sort if desired

Don't forget

This places the column of country names adjacent to the columns of surface area and population values, ready for further analysis, creating a chart for example. To help with this, you can sort the information, e.g. in descending order of population size.

Create a Chart

1 Highlight the data (including headers), then select the Insert tab and click the arrow on the Charts group

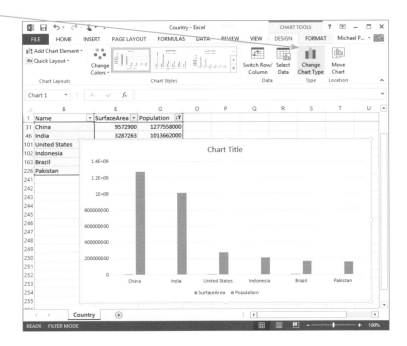

Hot tip

When you've created a chart, the Chart Tools Design and Format tabs are displayed, and you can select the Change Chart Type button to try one of the other options.

2 Choose the chart type and subtype, in this case, Column and Clustered Column

Beware

The Surface Area values are numerically much smaller than the Population values, so are very close to the horizontal axis and almost invisible. However, you can choose a secondary axis for the population values to make both sets of values visible.

3 Click one of the Population columns and select Format Data Series...

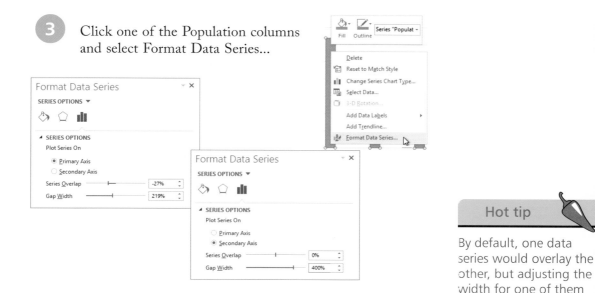

4 Choose Plot Series On Secondary Axis, and adjust Gap Width to 400%

5 Use the Chart Tools Format tab and Add Chart Element to edit, format and position the titles for the chart, the axes and the legend

Hot tip

By default, one data series would overlay the other, but adjusting the width for one of them allows you to view both sets of data together.

Don't forget

Select the Move Chart button on the Design tab to place the chart on a separate worksheet.

Import a List

Don't forget

In the sample worksheet, the Capital is shown as a City ID that references an external table of city names and other details.

The Country worksheet used as an example includes the Capital column, which provides a link to a list of cities. This list is available as a text file, so it can be imported into the worksheet.

1 Select a cell marking the start of an empty section of the worksheet, and then click the Data tab

2 Click Get External Data and choose From Text

Don't forget

The text is transferred into the worksheet as a named range, using the name of the external text file, e.g. City.

3 Locate the text file, click Import, then apply the Text Import Wizard (see page 86)

4 Click OK to place the data in the current worksheet, at the location selected initially

Create a Table

1 Click a cell within the data range and select the Insert tab, then click the Table button

Hot tip

To make it easier to manage and analyze the data in the list, you can turn the range of cells into an Excel table.

2 Click Yes to confirm the range and accept the headers

Don't forget

When you create a table from a data range, any connection with the external data source will be removed.

3 The table will be created (using the default style)

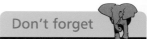

Hot tip

Change the default name (Table1 or similar) to something that's more relevant to the content, such as City.

Add Totals to Table

Hot tip

Convert the range of country data into table form, then add totals.

1 Click a cell within the country data and select Insert, Table, then rename the new table as Country

2 Select the Table Tools Design tab, then click the box for the Total Row, which is displayed at the end of the table

Don't forget

The functions that you choose are entered as subfunctions of Subtotal:

SUBTOTAL(101, Average
        (102, Count numbers
        (103, Count
        (104, Max
        (105, Min
        (107, StdDev
        (109, Sum
        (110, Variance

3 Select the Total box for Name, click the arrow and choose the appropriate function, e.g. Count

4 Select the Sum function for columns with numerical values, such as SurfaceArea, Population, or GNP

CcountryCode	Name	Continent	Region	SurfaceArea	IndepYear
239 ZMB	Zambia	Africa	Eastern Africa	752618	1964
240 ZWE	Zimbabwe	Africa	Eastern Africa	390757	1980
241 Total		239		148956306.9	

E241 =SUBTOTAL(109,[SurfaceArea])

Country - Excel

Hot tip

You do not use the column and row labels to specify cells and ranges, you use the header name for the column (enclosed in square brackets).

5 You can combine functions, such as Min and Max, to show the range of values in a column, e.g. IndepYear

F241 =CONCATENATE("From ",SUBTOTAL(105,[IndepYear])," to ",SUBTOTAL(104,[IndepYear]))

CountryCode	Name	Continent	Region	SurfaceArea	IndepYear	Population	Life
239 ZMB	Zambia	Africa	Eastern Africa	752618	1964	9169000	
240 ZWE	Zimbabwe	Africa	Eastern Africa	390757	1980	11669000	
241 Total		239		148956306.9	From -1523 to 1994		

Country - Excel

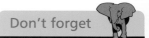

Don't forget

You can use any Excel function in the total boxes, not just the set of subfunctions in Subtotal.

6 When a column contains a set of discrete values, such as Continent or Region, you can calculate the number of unique values it contains

C241 {=SUM(1/COUNTIF([Continent],[Continent]))}

CountryCode	Name	Continent	Region	SurfaceArea	IndepYear
239 ZMB	Zambia	Africa	Eastern Africa	752618	1964
240 ZWE	Zimbabwe	Africa	Eastern Africa	390757	1980
241 Total		239	7	148956306.9	From -1523 to 1994

Country - Excel

This is an array formula that counts the number of times each particular value in the column is repeated, and uses these repeats to build up a count of the number of distinct values.

Hot tip

You type an array formula without the enclosing curly braces { }, then press Ctrl + Shift + Enter, instead of the usual Enter, and the braces are added automatically.

Computed Column

You can insert a column in the table without affecting other ranges, data or tables in the worksheet.

Hot tip

If you select a cell in the last column of the table, you can insert a column to the left or the right.

1 Click in the Population column, select the Home tab, click Insert, and choose Insert Table Columns to the Left

2 The new column is inserted and initially named Column1

Don't forget

The column names are used in the formulas, so it is best to choose meaningful names.

3 Select the new column header, type a new name, such as Density, and press Enter

4 Click in the first cell of the column, and type =, then click
the Population cell in the same row

Hot tip

The cell that you select is referenced as the current row of Population, in the form: [@Population].

5 Type /, then click the SurfaceArea cell in the same row

Hot tip

The next cell you select is referenced as: [@SurfaceArea].

6 Press Enter, the expression is evaluated and copied to all
the other cells in the table column

Don't forget

The result is the population density, the number of people per square kilometer. You can format the values in the cells, for example as two decimal places.

G
Density
34.84
118.31
13.21
341.71
166.67
10.33

Don't forget

The formula in each cell refers to [@ColName], which is the current row for the named column.

101

Table Lookup

The Country table contains a city code number for the capital city of each country, rather than the actual city name.

The names are stored in the separate City table, which has details of more than 4000 cities.

Hot tip

You can look up values in a table, and insert them in another table or data range.

To display the name of the capital city alongside the city number, in the Country table:

1 Insert a table column next to the Capital column and change its name to CapitalCity

Hot tip

Click in the adjacent Code2 column and apply Insert Table Columns to the Left (see page 100).

Don't forget

VLOOKUP is the vertical-lookup function, used when the values are stored in columns.

2 Click the first cell of the new column and type the expression =VLOOKUP(

3 Click the adjacent cell in the Capital column, then type the expression ,City,2,0)

The table reference [@Capital] is the Capital number from the current row. The other parameters are City (the table name), 2 (the column with the actual name) and 0 (the code for Exact Match).

Hot tip

4 Press Enter, and the capital city name is inserted on all the rows in the Country table, not just the current row

5 Scroll down to check the entries for particular countries, the United States (Washington) or the United Kingdom (London), for example

CountryCode	Name	Continent	Capital	CapitalCity	Code2
223 UKR	Ukraine	Europe		3426 Kyiv	UA
224 ARE	United Arab Emirat	Asia		65 Abu Dhabi	AE
225 GBR	United Kingdom	Europe		456 London	GB
226 USA	United States	North America		3813 Washington	US
227 UMI	United States Minc	Oceania		#N/A	UM
228 URY	Uruguay	South America		3492 Montevideo	UY
229 UZB	Uzbekistan	Asia		3503 Toskent	UZ
230 VUT	Vanuatu	Oceania		3537 Port-Vila	VU
231 VEN	Venezuela	South America		3539 Caracas	VE
232 VNM	Vietnam	Asia		3770 Hanoi	VN
233 VGB	Virgin Islands, Briti	North America		537 Road Town	VG
234 VIR	Virgin Islands, U.S.	North America		4067 Charlotte Ama	VI

Beware

If the area does not have a capital city (e.g. United States Minor Outlying Islands) then the value #N/A is entered, to show no match found.

Manage Data Using Access

If you have large amounts of data, or complex functions to handle, you may require the more comprehensive facilities in Access 2013.

1 Select Access from the Start screen or the Taskbar, and you'll be greeted by a range of database templates

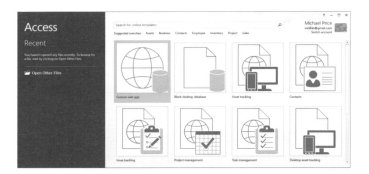

Hot tip

You'll find Access 2013 in the Professional editions of Office 2013. It appears as a tile on the Start screen, and you can also pin it to the Taskbar on the Desktop.

104

2 Select a category such as Assets to display a list of related templates available on the Internet

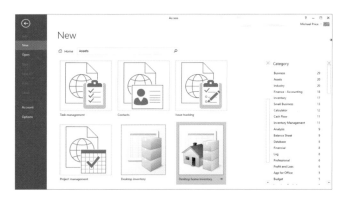

Hot tip

A default name such as Datebase1 will be assigned, but you can change this before you click the Create button.

File Name
Database1
C:\Users\Michael\Documents\

3 Select a template to view details

4 When you've found the template that you want to use, click the Create button

5 The selected template is downloaded to your computer

6 Access prepares the template for use as a new database

7 The database is opened with active content disabled

Don't forget

The template will be stored in the recent templates area and will be immediately available for reuse when you select File, New to create a database.

8 Click Enable Content to enable the VBA macros in the template and make the database ready for updating

Beware

Do not enable content in databases that you download from Internet websites, unless you are sure that the source of the file is trustworthy.

Add Records

Hot tip

You can type directly into the cells of the asset table if you wish, rather than using the form.

Hot tip

You can attach links to associated documents, or display a photograph of the asset, if you wish. Click the Attachments box and select Manage Attachments.

Don't forget

The current record is automatically saved when you click Close, even if all the details are not completed.

1 Click the New Asset button to add an entry to the Current Assets database

2 Enter the details for the item, selecting from a list of values on fields with an arrow, e.g. Category

3 Click Save and New, to save the current record and then begin a new record, or click Close to return to the list

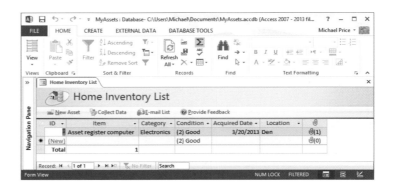

6 Presentations

Build a presentation, slide by slide, apply themes to create a consistent effect, and use animation to focus attention on particular points. Use a second monitor for a presenter view. Take advantage of templates, built-in or downloaded, and print handouts for the presentation. Rehearse the show, to get timings, and create an automatic show.

Start a Presentation

To start PowerPoint and create a presentation:

1 Select the PowerPoint tile on the Start screen or the icon on the Taskbar

Hot tip

When PowerPoint opens, it presents a single blank title slide, ready for you to begin a new presentation.

2 Select the Blank Presentation and Click to add title, then type the title for your slide show, e.g. Origami

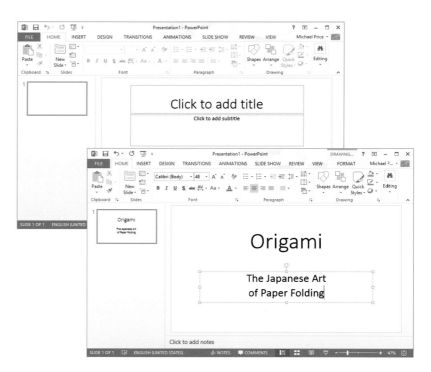

Don't forget

By default, the presentation starts with a title slide, where two text boxes are predefined. If you don't want a particular text box, just ignore it – it won't appear on the slide unless you edit the text.

3 Click to add subtitle, and type the subtitle for your slide show, e.g. The Japanese Art of Paper Folding

4 Select the Home tab and click the New Slide button in the Slides group

5 A new slide, with text boxes for title and content, will be added to the slide show

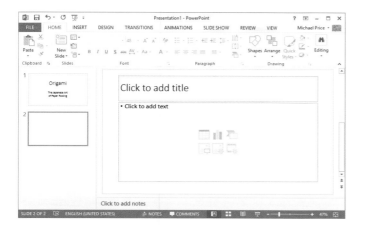

Hot tip

The new slide has option buttons to insert a table, chart, SmartArt graphic, or picture from a file, clip art or media clip. See page 111 for an example.

6 Click on the prompts and add the title The History of Origami, then type bullet points to give the details

7 Press Enter to add a new bullet item, and then press the Tab key to move to the next lower level of bullet items

Don't forget

Click within a bullet item and press Shift + Tab to move it up (promote it) to the next higher level.

Expand the Slide

1 Click the button to Save your presentation

2 Continue to add items, you'll see the text size and spacing adjusted to fit the text onto the slide

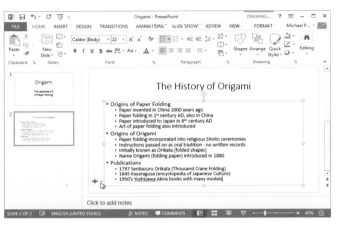

Don't forget

Alternatively, you can choose to stop fitting text to the placeholder, to continue on a new slide, or to change to a two-column format.

3 Click the AutoFit Options button that appears when the slide fills, and click Split Text Between Two Slides

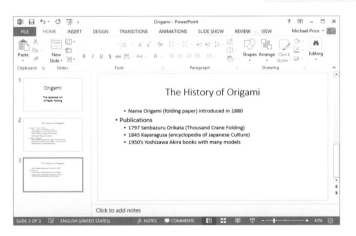

Hot tip

The text size and spacing will be re-adjusted to take advantage of the extra space available.

4 A new slide is inserted, with the same layout and title as the original slide, with bullet items shared between them

Insert a Picture

1 Select the Home tab, then click the arrow on the New Slide button in the Slides group to display the options

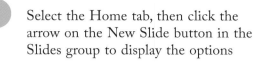

2 Choose a slide layout, such as Picture with Caption

3 Click the icon to add the picture

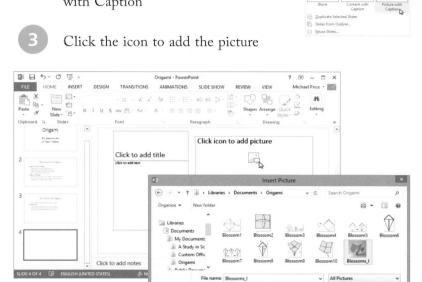

4 Locate and select the image file and click Insert, then select in turn Click to add title, and Click to add text

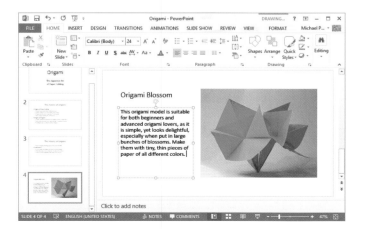

111

Hot tip

There are nine standard layouts for slides, so you can select the one that's most appropriate for the specific content planned for each slide.

Don't forget

The title and the text you add provide the caption for the inserted image.

Don't forget

Insert the other slides needed to complete your presentation.

Apply a Theme

The default slides have a plain background, but you can choose a more effective theme, and apply it to all the slides you've created.

1 Select the Design tab, and move the mouse pointer over each of the themes, to see the effect

Hot tip

The selected theme is temporarily applied to the current slide, to help you choose the most effective theme.

2 You can scroll the list to display additional themes, change the colors, fonts, and effects for the current theme, and modify the type of background style it uses

Don't forget

You can right-click your selected theme and choose to apply it to selected slides, or set the theme as the default for future slides.

3 Click the preferred theme to apply it to all of the slides in the presentation

To select the transition effects between slides:

1 Select the Transitions tab and review the options – starting with None, Cut, Fade, Push

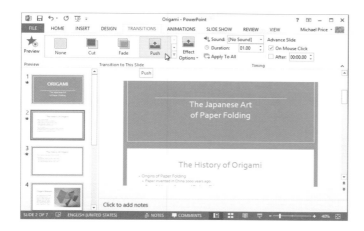

Hot tip

Move the mouse pointer over an effect to see it demonstrated on the current slide, e.g. Push from bottom.

2 Click the up and down arrows to view another of the 12 rows of effects

3 Click an effect to assign it to the current slide

By default, each slide advances to the next slide when you press the mouse key, but you can adjust the setting for individual slides.

4 Clear the On Mouse Click box to disable the mouse-key for the current slide

Don't forget

When you select a transition, the Effects Options button is enabled, so you can choose variations of that transition.

5 Select to Advance Slide After the specified time

6 Click the Apply To All button to apply the settings to all the slides in the presentation

Whatever the setting, you can always advance the slide show by pressing one of the keyboard shortcuts, such as N (next), Enter, Page Down, right arrow, or spacebar.

Don't forget

If you have specified animation effects for individual elements on a slide (see page 114), the Advance function invokes the next animation, rather than the next slide.

Animations

You can apply animation effects to individual parts of a slide.

Don't forget

The animation can be at Entrance, for Emphasis, or at Exit, and may be applied All At Once or By 1st Level Paragraph.

1 Select the Animations tab, pick a slide with bullet items, and note that the Animate button is grayed (inactive)

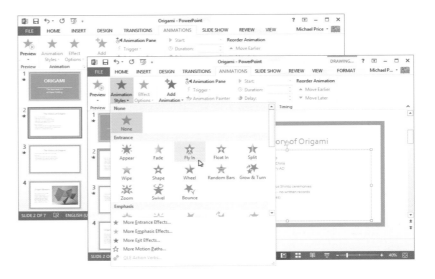

Beware

If you specify animation within the slide, you may want to enable automatic advance, unless you plan to manually display each line of the slide.

114

2 Select the text box with the bullet items, and the Animate button is activated

3 Click the down arrow on the Animate box and choose, for example, Fly In, By 1st Level Paragraph, then click the Preview button to observe the effect

Hot tip

Select Add Animation in the Advanced Animation group, if you want to apply additional effects to the slide.

Run the Show

When you've added all the slides you need, you can try running the complete show, to see the overall effect.

1 Select the Slide Show tab and click the From the Beginning button in the Start Slide Show group

2 The slides are displayed full-screen, with the transition and animation effects that you selected

The History of Origami

- Origins of Paper Folding
  - Paper invented in China 2000 years ago
  - Paper folding in 1st century AD, also in China
  - Paper introduced to Japan in 6th century AD
  - Art of paper folding also Introduced

- Origins of Origami
  - Paper folding incorporated into religious Shinto ceremonies
  - Instructions passed on as oral tradition - no written records
  - Initially known as Orikata (folded shapes)

3 Click the mouse or keyboard shortcut to advance the slide show, animation by animation, or wait the specified time

4 Review each slide in turn to the end of the show

Hot tip

You can also press F5 to run the slide show from the beginning, press Shift + F5 to run from the current slide, or press Esc to terminate.

Don't forget

You'll see the selected transition effect between the slides, in this example the effect is Dissolve.

Hot tip

When the slide show finishes, a black screen is presented, with the message: End of slide show, click to exit.

End of slide show, click to exit.

Other Views

Hot tip

This view is very helpful when you have a larger number of slides, since you can simply drag slides into their new positions.

1 Select the View tab and select Slide Sorter to display all the slides, so that you can rearrange their sequence

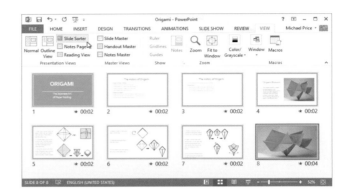

Don't forget

Each slide and its notes will be displayed on a single sheet, which can be printed to make a very useful handout.

2 Select the Notes Page view to see the current slide with its notes (information and prompts for the presenter)

Hot tip

There's also a Reading View button, provided in the Presentation Views group on the Views tab, which allows you to view the slide show.

3 Click the Zoom button and select a zoom level then click OK (or drag the slider on the zoom bar), to examine the slide or notes in detail

4 Select Fit and click OK (or click the Fit to Window button) to resize the view, to make the whole page visible

5 To switch back to the view with slide bar and current slide, click the Normal button

Beware

The view you select will be retained when you select another tab, so you should revert to the required view before leaving.

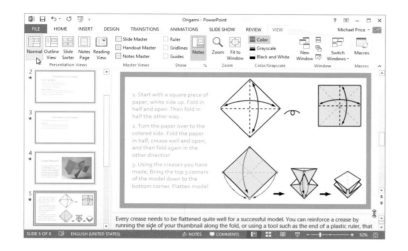

6 To reveal more of the notes area, click and drag the separator bar upwards

7 Click the Outline tab to see the text content of the slides, giving a summary view of the presentation

Hot tip

The buttons to the left of the Zoom bar are another way to select Normal, Slide Sorter, Reading, and Slide Show views

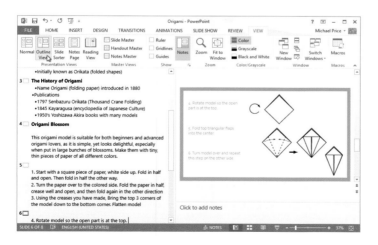

8 Scroll the summary area as needed to view all the slides

Presenter View

Hot tip

If your system has dual-monitor support, you can run your presentation from one monitor, while your audience views it on a second monitor (or on a projector screen).

1 Select the Slide Show tab, and click the box to enable the Use Presenter View option

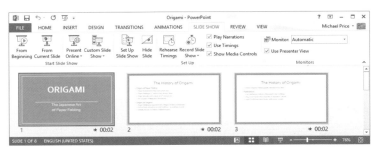

2 If you have attached a second monitor, right-click the desktop and select Screen Resolution

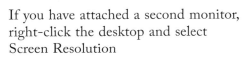

3 Click the Multiple Displays box and select Extend these displays

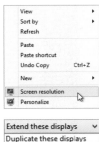

Don't forget

When you change your display settings, you must confirm to keep the changes within 15 seconds or the changes will be reversed.

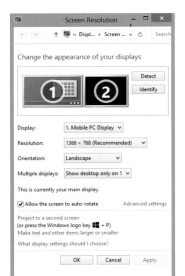

4 Click Apply, then OK and click Keep Changes when prompted

5 Select the Slide Show tab and click From Beginning to run the slide show on the two monitors

The first monitor gives the presenter's view, with the current slide and its associated notes, plus a preview of the next slide. There's also a Slide bar, to change the sequence of slides during the show.

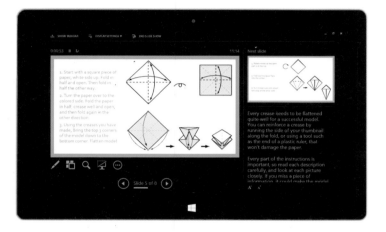

The second monitor is for your audience and displays the current slides in full-screen mode.

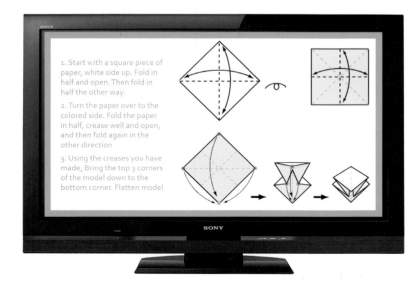

Don't forget

If you do not have a second monitor or projector attached you can still select Presenter View and press Alt + F5 to run the show from the presenter's view only.

119

Hot tip

Use the Zoom button to enlarge the notes and make them easier to read while giving the presentation.

Choose a Template

Hot tip

Templates provide ready-built presentations, which can be adapted to your needs. They also offer examples of useful PowerPoint techniques.

1 Select the File tab, then click New, to display the example templates provided

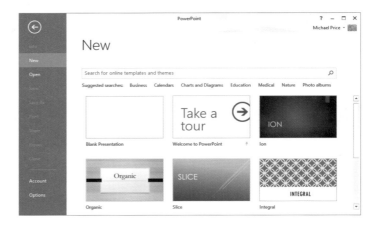

2 Select a template, for example Slice, to see details and view images using the themes and colors offered

3 To make a presentation using the template, click Create, otherwise close the overview and review other templates

4 You can use one of the suggested categories, for example Business, to search for online templates and themes

Don't forget

You can also enter your own keywords if you want to make a more specific search for suitable templates.

5 PowerPoint searches online for relevant templates and themes

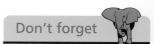

6 Thumbnails and links are displayed for the items located, and the associated subcategories are also listed

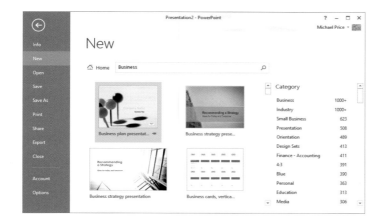

Don't forget

PowerPoint shows the number of templates in each subcategory, and you can select these to identify more closely a suitable template.

121

7 Select, for example, the Business plan presentation, and you'll see it consists of twelve slides on various topics

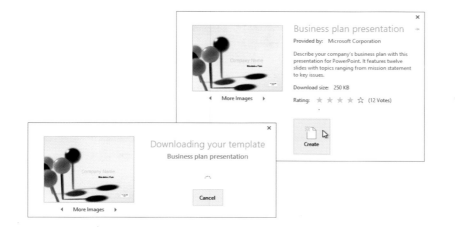

Hot tip

The Templates that you download and review will be added to the templates displayed when you select File, New in future sessions.

8 Click Create and the template will be downloaded and a presentation based on it will be opened

Use the Template

1 When you create a new presentation with a template, it opens showing the predefined slides and content

Don't forget

You can revise the text, add and replace images with your own pictures, and make your own presentation based on the template.

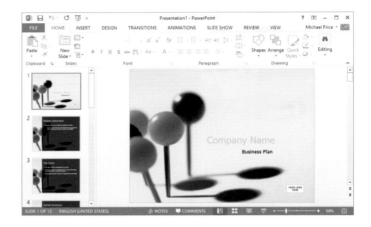

2 You can edit any of the slides, remove unnecessary slides or add new slides (using the same theme if desired)

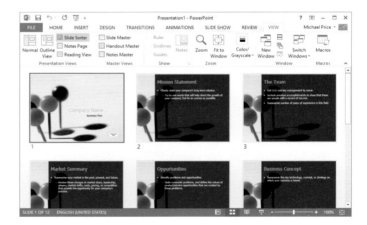

Don't forget

The template will be retained in its original form in case you want to use it again in the future.

3 To make it easier to resequence the slides, select View and click Slide Sorter

4 Save the presentation, with a new name to preserve the changes

Print the Slide Show

1 Select the File tab, then click the Print button to specify the printer and other printing options

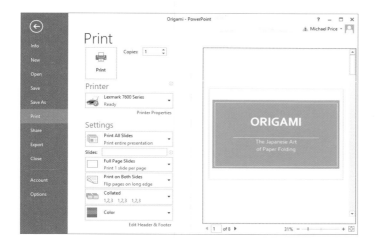

Print Preview is provided, and you can use the scroll bar to view the slides in your presentation. The Zoom bar allows you to take a closer view.

2 Select the printer you want to use, or accept the default

Don't forget

You can choose to print the document in grayscale, or pure black-and-white, even if the presentation itself is in full color.

3 Enter slide numbers or ranges, and the Print All Slides setting changes to Custom Range

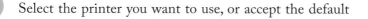

4 Click the Print Layout button to choose what type of document to print

5 You can print full page slides, slides with notes, or an outline

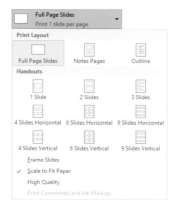

6 If you select Handouts, you can specify the number of slides to a page, and the order (horizontal or vertical)

7 You can also select Frames Slides, Scale to Fit Paper, and High Quality printing

Rehearse Timings

Hot tip

You can make the presentation easier to run by assigning timings to the slides, so that it can run automatically.

Don't forget

The timer shows the duration so far for the individual slide, and for the presentation as a whole.

Hot tip

Select the Transitions tab to make further adjustments to the times for particular slides.

To establish the timings for each slide, you need to rehearse the presentation and record the times for each step.

1. Select the Slide Show tab and click Rehearse Timings, which is in the Set Up group

2. The slide show runs full-screen in manual mode, with the timer superimposed in the top left corner

3. Advance each slide or animation, allowing for viewing and narration, etc., and the times will be recorded

4. When the presentation finishes, you can choose to keep the new slide timings for the next time you view the show

5. The view changes to Slide Sorter, with individual times for the slides. Make sure that Use Timings is selected

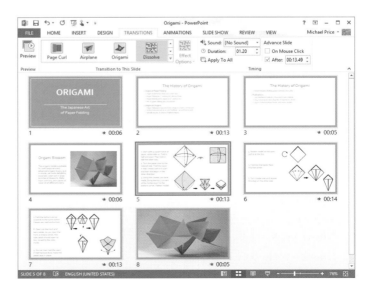

Save As Options

1 Select the File tab and the Info view is selected, with all the details of the presentation file

2 Click Save As, and then click the box labelled Save as type, to see what file formats are supported

3 The PowerPoint Presentation (.pptx) format is the default, and is the file type that is designed for editing the presentation

4 Select the PowerPoint Show (.ppsx) format for the file type that is protected from modification. This will open in the Slide Show view

Hot tip

There are several forms you can save your PowerPoint 2013 Presentation in, including ways to share it with other users.

Don't forget

Save in the PowerPoint 97–2003 Show format (or Presentation format), to allow users with older versions of PowerPoint to view (or modify) the presentation.

Package for CD

1 With the required presentation open, select the File tab, Save & Send, and then Package Presentation for CD

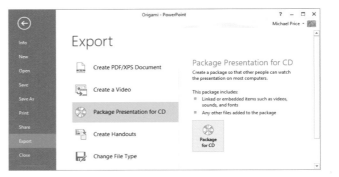

Hot tip

You can also create a PDF or XMS document or create a video of the presentation, to send as email attachments perhaps, or create printed handouts.

2 Type a name for the CD, add more presentations, if required, then click Copy to Folder

3 Edit the folder name and location, if necessary, then click OK

Don't forget

The package will include any linked or embedded items required, such as videos, sounds and fonts.

4 The presentation files are added to the folder, along with all the files needed to run the PowerPoint Viewer

5 Confirm that you have everything you need, then go back to the Package for CD window (see step 2) and this time select Copy to CD. You'll be prompted to insert a blank CD, and the files will be added

7 Office Extras

OneNote is an extra application that is becoming mainstream. There are other extras included with all editions of Office, such as Office Tools for managing and maintaining your copy of Office, though some tools are being superseded by apps from Windows Store.

OneNote 2013

OneNote is the digital version of a pocket notebook, giving you the means to capture, organize, and access all of the information you need for a specific task or project, personal or collaborative, and in whatever the format of the data – typed, written, audio, video, figures, or photographs.

The first version, OneNote 2003 was a stand-alone product. The next version OneNote 2007 was in three of the Office 2007 editions. OneNote 2010 was all Office 2010 editions except Starter. OneNote 2013 is in all editions of Office 2013 including Office RT, Office 365 and the online Office Web Apps.

To start using OneNote 2013 on your computer:

1. Select the OneNote tile from the Start screen, or click the OneNote icon on the Taskbar

2. OneNote starts up and opens your initial notebook called My Notebook, with the Quick Notes section selected and the advice page OneNote: one place for all your notes

This covers topics such as:

- Take notes anywhere on the page
- Get organized and add sections and pages
- For more tips, review the 30-second videos
- Create your first page in the Quick Notes section

Don't forget

A later addition to the set of products in the various versions of the Microsoft Office suites, OneNote is now fully incorporated in all the Office 2013 editions.

Hot tip

OneNote offers four 30-second videos on these useful topics:
1. Clip from the Web
2. Plan a trip with others
3. Search notes instantly
4. Write notes on slides

3 Select the second advice page OneNote Basics

Hot tip

The first time it starts, OneNote copies folder OneNote Notebooks (containing the Personal notebook) to your Documents Library.

This covers additional topics including:

- Remember everything
- Collaborate with others
- Organize with tables
- Integrate with Outlook
- Add Excel spreadsheets
- Brainstorm without clutter

4 When you display this page you'll see a second OneNote icon on the Taskbar, with the Send to OneNote tool

Hot tip

If the Send to OneNote is not displayed, select View and then click the button for Send to OneNote Tool in the Windows group.

5 Click in the box if you want this tool to always be loaded when you start OneNote

Create a Notebook

You can create a new OneNote notebook from scratch:

 Open OneNote and select the File tab, then click New

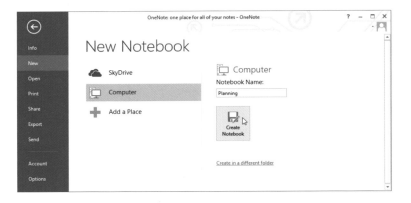

Hot tip

The default location for Computer is the OneNote Notebooks subfolder, in the Documents folder for the active user name.

 Choose where to put the notebook (SkyDrive, Computer or Add a Place) and provide the name, e.g. Planning

 Edit the location, if necessary, then click Create Notebook

Don't forget

OneNote doesn't provide any content for you or offer any templates by default, though you can locate OneNote templates at the Office website.

The notebook opens with a new section and an untitled page, ready for you to add notes, new pages, and new sections, or to send documents or clips from other applications.

As with most Office applications, you will find it easier and more instructive to start from a suitable template.

1 Select the Help icon on the Title bar at the right (or press F1)

2 Select More in the Getting started section

3 Internet Explorer opens **office.microsoft.com** at the web page Get started with OneNote 2013

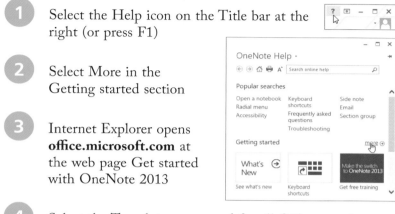

Hot tip

With OneNote, you need to visit the Office.com or other websites to find templates. They are not shown when you select File, New to create a notebook.

4 Select the Templates command for all Office templates

5 Select More, OneNote to display related templates

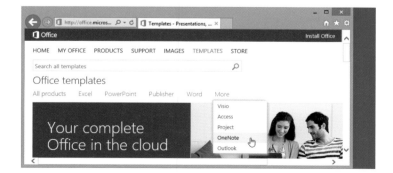

Don't forget

The Template command shows templates for all the Office applications, so you need to select the specific application to restrict the list to relevant templates only.

Download a Template

1   The Office website offers many templates for OneNote

Don't forget

There are templates for all versions of OneNote, and these can all be used with OneNote 2013.

Hot tip

You may get a message saying that a Pop-up has been blocked. Click the message and select to allow pop-ups. If you are not sure of the site, choose Allow once.

2   Select a suitable template to view its details, then click Download to add it to your system

Home improvement journal
OneNote 2010

3   Amend name or location if desired and click Save

4   Click Create to unpack and open the notebook

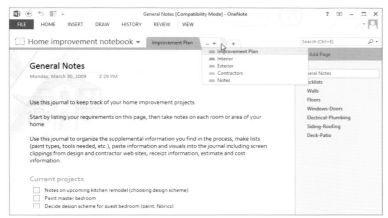

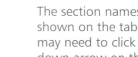
Don't forget

The section names are shown on the tabs. You may need to click the down arrow on the tab bar to display the rest of the sections.

The template is based on an older version of OneNote so opens in compatibility mode. To change the format of the new notebook:

1 Right-click the Notebook tab and select Properties

Hot tip

If you are sharing the notebook with users of an older OneNote, you may not want to convert to the newer version.

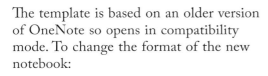

2 Click Convert to 2010-2013 and the file will be converted to the latest format and saved

Don't forget

Once you've opened or created a notebook, it will be reopened every time OneNote starts, unless you select File, Info, right-click Settings for that notebook, and select Close.

OneNote App

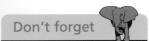

Don't forget

There's a Windows 8 app that allows access to notebooks on the SkyDrive. This makes it easy to share notebooks with computers that do not have a copy of Microsoft Office installed.

You can read and create notebooks on your Windows 8 computer, even if it doesn't have a copy of Microsoft Office, if you install the Windows 8 OneNote app.

1 Visit the Windows Store from the Start screen and search for OneNote apps, then select the Productivity category

2 Select the free OneNote app to review the details

Hot tip

This OneNote app can be installed on Windows RT computers as well as Windows 8 computers. There are equivalent apps available for mobile devices such as the Windows Phones.

3 Select the Install button to download the app and install it on your system

4 A tile is added to the Start screen

5 Select the new OneNote tile and the Windows 8 app starts with an initial notebook containing helpful advice

Don't forget

There's no Ribbon in the OneNote app but you can touch or click the button to display the Radial Menu which is particularly designed for touch interactions.

6 Select the video link to view an introduction which emphasizes that it keeps everything on the SkyDrive

All your notes in the cloud.

7 Right-click or swipe up on the OneNote screen and select Notebooks from the Apps bar to list any other notebooks that may be stored on your SkyDrive

Hot tip

You can also access the notebooks in your SkyDrive using the Web App version of OneNote (see page 230).

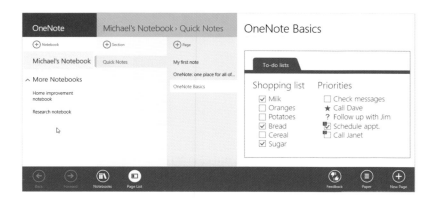

Office Tools

Hot tip

The Office suite includes a set of tools, as well as applications. You can check which tools have been installed on your system.

Don't forget

The tools available vary by edition. These are the tools in Office 2013 Professional Plus. Other editions may have fewer tools. The Office 2013 student edition in Windows RT, for example, has just two (Language Preferences and Upload Center).

To see which Office tools are already installed on your system:

1 Right-click the Windows 8 Start screen and select All apps from the Apps bar

2 Right-click an Office 2013 tool such as the Upload Center and select Open file location from the Apps bar

3 You'll find shortcuts for the installed Office tools, in the folder C:\ProgramData\Microsoft\Windows\Start Menu\ Programs\Microsoft Office 2013\Office 2013 Tools\

You can check to see what other tools may be included with your edition of Office 2013.

1 From the Desktop, display the Charms bar, select Settings. then select Control Panel

2 Locate the Programs category and click Uninstall a program. This option also provides facilities to Add, Change or Repair programs

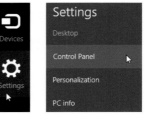

3 Select the entry for Microsoft Office and click Change

Hot tip

You can use Uninstall a program to explore the Office 2013 configuration options for all editions of Office 2013 except Office 2013 RT, which is installed as part of the Windows RT operating system.

4 Select Add or Remove Features and click Continue

137

6 Scroll the installation options and review the entries for Office Shared Features and the Office Tools

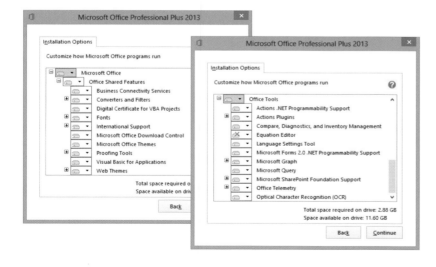

Don't forget

If any of the Shared Features or Tools are shown as not installed, you can select Run from my computer and allow Configuration to complete the installation.

Otherwise, just Close and Cancel the Configuration.

7 When you've selected all that you want, click [X] to Close

Language Preferences

Don't forget

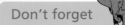

Office supports multiple languages, for editing, for display, for help, and for screen tips.

1. This document includes text in French, which confuses the default English (United States) spelling checker

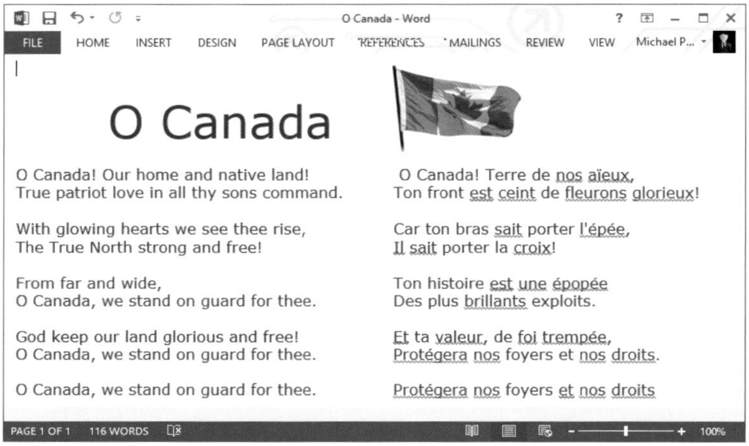

You'll have similar problems whenever you need to work with documents that have text in other languages, or when you use a system with a different language installed, e.g. when traveling.

To check which languages are enabled, and to add a new language:

1. From the Start screen, display the All apps screen and select Office Language Preferences

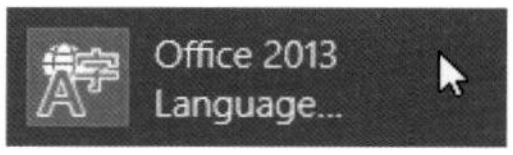

2. Click the Add Languages box and choose the language

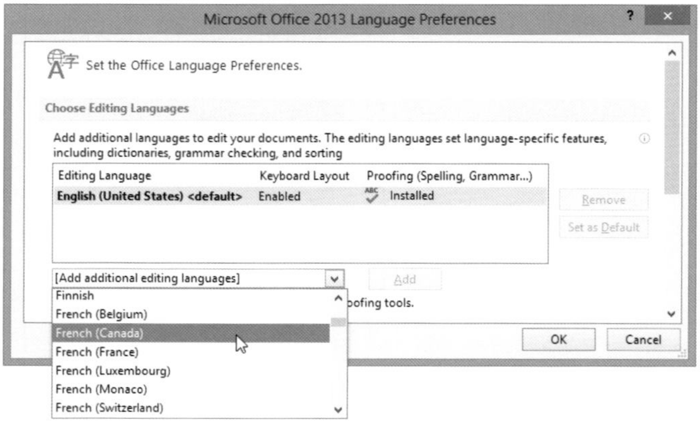

Hot tip

You can also set Office language preferences, by selecting File, Options, Language, from within any Office application.

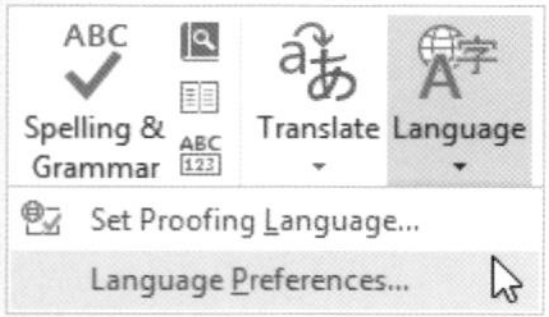

3 Click the Add button, then select  any other languages you require, and add them in turn

Don't forget

You may be required to enable an appropriate keyboard layout for the language you choose.

4 Click OK, then OK again to apply the changes, then close and restart any Office applications that are open

5 Any text in the new languages will normally be detected, and the appropriate spell checker will be employed

O Canada

O Canada! Our home and native land!
True patriot love in all thy sons command.

With glowing hearts we see thee rise,
The True North strong and free!

From far and wide,
O Canada, we stand on guard for thee.

God keep our land glorious and free!
O Canada, we stand on guard for thee.

O Canada, we stand on guard for thee.

O Canada! Terre de nos aïeux,
Ton front est ceint de fleurons glorieux!

Car ton bras sait porter l'épée,
Il sait porter la croix!

Ton histoire est une épopée
Des plus brillants exploits.

Et ta valeur, de foi trempée,
Protégera nos foyers et nos droits.

Protégera nos foyers et nos droits

Hot tip

If required, you can select any portions of the text not properly detected, then click Review, Language, Set Proofing Language, and make the appropriate choice.

Compare Spreadsheets

The Spreadsheet Compare tool lets you pick any two workbooks and compare them very quickly. The differences between spreadsheets are categorized so you can focus on important changes, such as changes to formulas.

Hot tip

Spreadsheet Compare can determine, for example, when rows or columns have been inserted or deleted and report this rather than highlighting consequential differences in cell contents.

To see the tool in action:

1 Select Spreadsheet Compare from the All apps screen

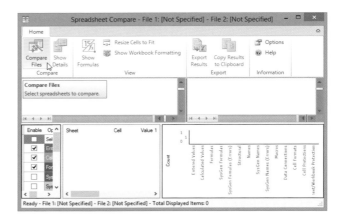

2 Click the button to Compare Files

Don't forget

You might choose two versions of the same spreadsheet to identify amendments that may have been made, or two spreadsheets with similar contents, in this case country populations in 2000 and 2013.

3 Select the Browse buttons in turn to locate the two spreadsheets that you'd like to compare

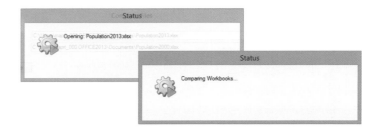

4 The two workbooks are opened and compared, and the results are displayed side-by-side

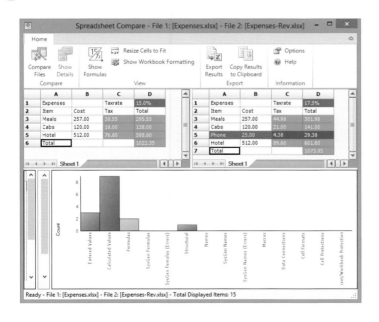

Hot tip

In this example it's only data values (populations, ranks and some country names) that are flagged as different.

Hot tip

You can choose to display the formulas in each cell rather than the values, to help identify possible causes for changes.

Show Formulas

5 Spreadsheet Compare can identify more complex changes

Don't forget

Here the tax rate has changed, and an extra line has been entered. The tool understands that some items get displaced, and only flags the actual differences, e.g. in the tax and the totals.

Database Compare

You may need to install some developments tools such as Microsoft.NET Framework and Microsoft Report Viewer before you can run the Database Compare tool.

This tool provides facilities for comparing the structures of different versions of an Access database.

 Select the Database Compare tool from the All apps screen

 Specify the Access databases that you wish to compare, and choose which elements to reviewed

Click Compare, and the database comparison report is generated

The reports concentrate on changes to the design of the tables, queries and other components, rather than changes to the data content of the tables. This allows you to identify changes made by others if the support of the database is shared.

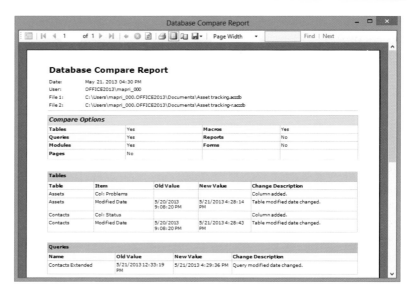

Other Tools

The following tools may also be included in your edition of Office:

Office Upload Center

This allows you to check the status of files
that get uploaded to web servers (your
SkyDrive for example). Microsoft Office first saves such files
locally in the Office Document Cache before it starts the upload,
which means that you can save changes and continue working
even when you are offline or have a slow network connection. The
Microsoft Office Upload Center lets you keep track of progress,
and whether any files need attention.

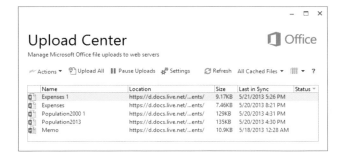

Telemetry Dashboard and Telemetry Log

Office Telemetry is a new compatibility
monitoring framework. When an Office
document or solution is loaded, used,
closed, or raises an error in Office 2013
applications, the application adds a
record about the event to the Telemetry
Log associated with each user. Inventory and usage data is also
tracked. The Telemetry Dashboard amalgamates the information
for all the users so that the technical administrator can assess the
compatibility of the whole system.

Lync Recording Manager

This is used with the Lync 2013
application (see page 224) to manage
the recordings of online meetings
and conferences conducted using the instant messaging and
communications facilities that are built into Lync. It is intended
for the business environment and requires the Microsoft
Exchange Server for full function.

This is used with the Lync 2013
application (see page 224) to manage

Hot tip

The Document Cache
and the Upload Center
are very useful when you
are traveling and do not
always have access to the
Internet.

Don't forget

Office Telemetry is a
sophisticated system
that is based on Excel
2013 workbooks but also
requires access to an SQL
Server.

Tools Removed from Office

A number of the tools that were previously included with Office have been removed, often being replaced by alternative features included in the Office applications, or by tools and utilities that are available elsewhere. For example:

Microsoft Binder

This was designed as a container system for storing related documents in a single file, but was discontinued after Office XP. OneNote offers similar, though more comprehensive, functions.

Microsoft Office Document Image Writer

This was a virtual printer for documents from Microsoft Office and other application to store them in TIFF or Microsoft Document Imaging Format. It was discontinued with Office 2010.

Microsoft Office Document Imaging

This allowed you to edit scanned documents. It was discontinued with Office 2010.

Microsoft Office Document Scanning

This scanning and OCR (Optical Character Recognition) application was discontinued with Office 2010. However, OCR facilities are included in OneNote.

Microsoft Office Picture Manager

This provided photo management and enhancement software but with Office 2013 it has been removed. It has been replaced by the various Photos apps available from the Windows Store and by Windows Live Photo Gallery. This product is part of the Windows Essentials (see **http://windows.microsoft.com/en-us/windows-live/essentials**) which are available for Windows 8 but not Windows RT systems.

Clip Organizer

This was used to collect and store clip art, photos, animations, videos, and other media to use in documents, presentations, spreadsheets and other files. It was discontinued in Office 2013 and effectively replaced by the Insert Illustrations and Insert Media functions which let you find and insert content from online collections.

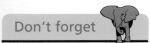
Don't forget

These are just some of the products that Microsoft has made available for a time as Office Tools, and then decided to remove or replace.

Don't forget

With Windows 8, the emphasis will be on apps provided through the Windows Store, so the facilities provided via the Office Tools can be expected to reduce further with future versions.

8 Email

The first time you use
Outlook, you may need to
specify your email account.
Then you can receive
messages, save attachments,
print messages, issue replies,
and update your address book,
while protecting yourself from
spam messages that might be
targeted at your account. You
can add a standard signature
note to your messages.
Outlook also helps you
subscribe to RSS feeds.

Starting Outlook

The Microsoft Outlook program provides the email and time management functions in Office 2013. To start the application:

 Display the Start screen and select the tile for Microsoft Outlook 2013

To make this application quicker and easier to find, you can add it as a shortcut on the Taskbar.

 Locate the Outlook entry on the Start screen, as described above, then right-click and select the Pin to Taskbar button

 The associated icon will be added to the Taskbar, beside any other applications you may already have selected

To start Microsoft Outlook from the Taskbar:

 With the Desktop displayed, click the Microsoft Outlook icon on the Taskbar and the application will be launched

Don't forget

Outlook 2013 is found in all editions of Office 2013 except the Home and Student edition (including the edition supplied with Windows RT 8.0). Systems with that edition would use the Mail app to send and receive email.

Hot tip

If you have Office 2013 Professional Plus or an Office 365 business edition, the Lync instant messaging application will also start up when you start Outlook.

The first time you start Outlook, it helps you to define the email accounts you want to manage using this application.

Outlook detects when no accounts are defined, and runs the Startup wizard to obtain details of your email account.

1 Click Next to get started, select Yes to set up Outlook to connect an email account, then click Next again

2 Type your name, your email address, and your password and click Next to set up your account automatically

You could manually configure your account, but the easiest way to add the account is to let the wizard establish the settings for you.

Configure Server Settings

Don't forget

Your email account may use POP3 connections, where messages are fully downloaded to your computer, or IMAP, where messages are listed on your computer but not downloaded until you open them.

1 The wizard identifies your Internet connection, and establishes the network connection

Add Account	✕

Searching for your mail server settings...

Configuring

Outlook is completing the setup for your account. This might take several minutes.

✓ Establishing network connection
➡ **Searching for maprice39@gmail.com settings**
Logging on to the mail server

< Back   Next >   Cancel

2 The wizard then searches for the server settings that support your email account

Add Account	✕

Searching for your mail server settings...

Configuring

Outlook is completing the setup for your account. This might take several minutes.

✓ Establishing network connection
✓ Searching for maprice39@gmail.com settings
➡ **Log on to server and send a test e-mail message**

< Back   Next >   Cancel

Hot tip

For some email accounts, those from Yahoo.com for example, the wizard may be unable to detect the settings. You will need to select the option to Change account settings and enter the information provided by your email supplier.

3 Finally, the wizard logs on to the server, using your account name and password, and sends a test message. Click Finish and your email account will be ready for use

Outlook is completing the setup for your account.
✓ Establishing network connection
✓ Searching for maprice@yahoo.com settings
✗ Log on to server and send a test e-mail message
We are having trouble connecting to your account.
☑ Change account settings

Add Account	✕

Congratulations!

Configuring

Outlook is completing the setup for your account. This might take several minutes.

✓ Establishing network connection
✓ Searching for maprice39@gmail.com settings
✓ Log on to server and send a test e-mail message

Your **IMAP** e-mail account is successfully configured.

☐ Change account settings   Add another account...

< Back   Finish   Cancel

Your First Messages

Outlook opens with the Inbox, showing your first email messages, e.g. welcome messages from the ISP, or the Outlook test message.

Quick Access Toolbar Tab bar Title bar Help

Ribbon

To-Do bar

Calendar

Appointment list

Task list

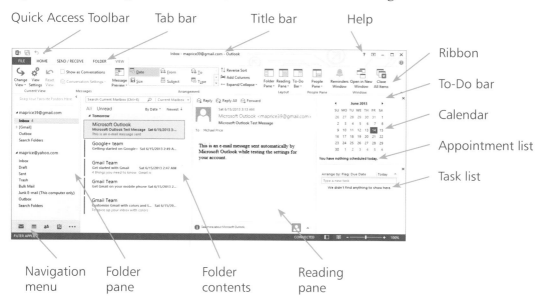

Navigation menu Folder pane Folder contents Reading pane

You may collapse the Folder pane and hide the To-Do bar, to provide more space to display more message content, or to cope with a smaller screen size. You may also position the Reading Pane below the message list, or hide it altogether (see page 150).

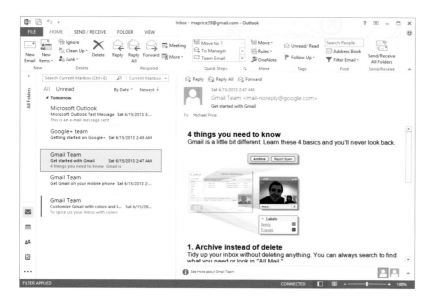

149

Hot tip

Outlook may prevent automatic download of some pictures in the message. If you trust the source, you can choose to download the pictures.

Turn Off Reading Pane

1 Select View, Reading Pane, and choose Off, rather than Right or Bottom

2 Messages will be left unread until opened

Hot tip

It is possible that the very act of reading an email message could release harmful software into your system. Turn off the Reading pane and review the message source and title before it is actually read, to avoid potential problems with spam and phishing emails (see pages 159-159).

Don't forget

The messages that have been opened are listed with regular rather than bold and colored font.

3 Double-click (or select and press Enter) to open a message and display its contents

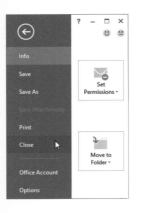

4 Click the Close button at the top right

5 Click the Up or Down arrows on the Quick Access toolbar to switch to the previous message or the next message

6 Alternatively, select File and then select Close from the action list in the back stage view

Request a Newsletter

You'll need to share your email address with friends, contacts, and organizations, to begin exchanging messages. You can also use your email address to request newsletters. For example:

 1 Visit the website **http://thrillerwriters.org/** and select ITW, The Big Thrill to see details of the newsletter

2 Scroll down to the form to apply for a subscription

3 Enter your email address, first name and last name, and choose the format required

4 Click the Subscribe button

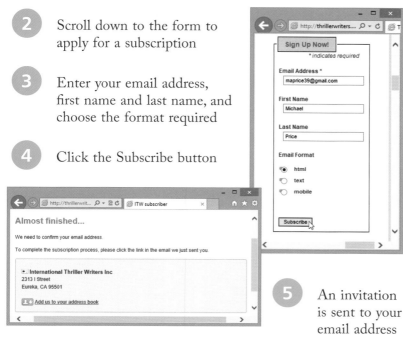

5 An invitation is sent to your email address

Hot tip

ITW is an honorary society of authors who write books, fiction and nonfiction, broadly classified as thrillers. The website features a regular newsletter.

Don't forget

There may be a fee for the service in some cases, though, most often, the newsletters are provided free of charge, as in this example.

...cont'd

6 Double-click the email confirmation request message when it arrives in your Inbox

Don't forget

Your address could be provided, accidently or deliberately, without your permission, so you must explicitly confirm you wish to subscribe.

7 Select the link provided, to confirm you issued the request

8 The website is updated to confirm the subscription

9 A further email will arrive in your Inbox, completing the subscription

Hot tip

Retain this email, since it provides the links needed to change your details, or to unsubscribe, if you no longer wish to receive the newsletter.

Receive a Message

To check for any mail that may be waiting:

1 Open Outlook, select the Send/Receive tab, and click the Send/Receive button

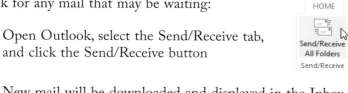

2 New mail will be downloaded and displayed in the Inbox

3 Double-click the message title to display the contents

 4 Right-click one of the attachments, and then select Save As to save that particular attachment

5 Specify the target folder (see page 154) and choose Save

Don't forget

Depending on the settings, Outlook may automatically issue a Send/Receive when it starts up, and at intervals thereafter. You can also manually check for messages at any time.

Hot tip

Select the Send/Receive tab to get extra functions that give more control over the Send/Receive process.

153

Save All Attachments

To save all the attachments at once:

Hot tip

This is the safest way to handle attachments, which can then be scanned by your antivirus checker before further processing.

1 Open the message, right-click any attachment, and select Save All Attachments...

2 The list of attachments is displayed, with all the attachments selected

3 Press Ctrl, and click any of the attachments to adjust the selection if desired, then click OK to download the files

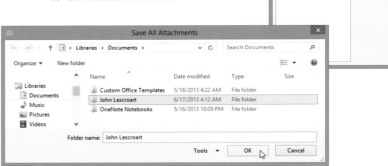

4 Locate the folder to receive the downloads (or click New Folder to insert a new folder), then click OK to save

Don't forget

Copies of the attachment will be retained in your Inbox, until you delete the associated message (and empty the Deleted Items folder).

5 Open the target folder in File Explorer to view the files that you have just saved

Print the Message

1 From the message, select the File tab, then click Print

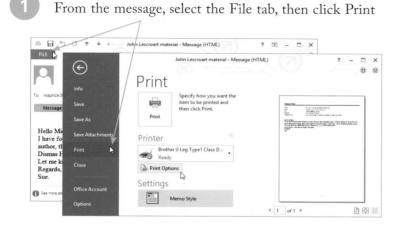

Hot tip

The File Print Preview shows how the message will appear on the page. Select Quick Print to send the message to the printer, using all the default settings.

2 Click Print Options to change the printer or adjust the print settings, e.g. the number of copies

3 When you click to select the Print options box, you can also print the file attachments (on the default printer only)

4 For picture attachments, you can choose the print size of the image

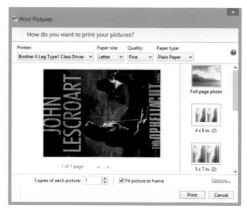

Beware

Each attachment will print as a separate print job, destined for the default printer. You can change the print size on each job, but you cannot combine the prints onto the same sheet.

Reply to the Message

1 When you want to reply to a message that you've opened, click the Reply button, in the Respond group on the Message tab

Hot tip

If there are other addressees, you can click Reply to All. If you want to share the message with another person, click Forward.

2 The message form opens with the email address, the subject entered, and the cursor in the message area, ready for you to type your comments above the original text

Don't forget

The Compose mode of the Message Editor has additional tabs – Insert, Options, Format Text, and Review.

3 Complete your response and then click the Send button to transfer the response initially to the Outbox and then to the Sent folder upon completion

Don't forget

The message is moved to the Outbox, and when it has been sent, a copy goes to Sent Items. A Sent note is attached to the original message, the message icon is updated, and Outlook can keep track of the conversation.

Note that the Reading Pane may be active in the Sent folder, even if it has been switched off in the Inbox, since the Reading Pane must be separately configured for each folder

Add Address to Contacts

Whenever you receive an email, you can add the email for the sender (and any other addressees) to your Outlook Contacts list

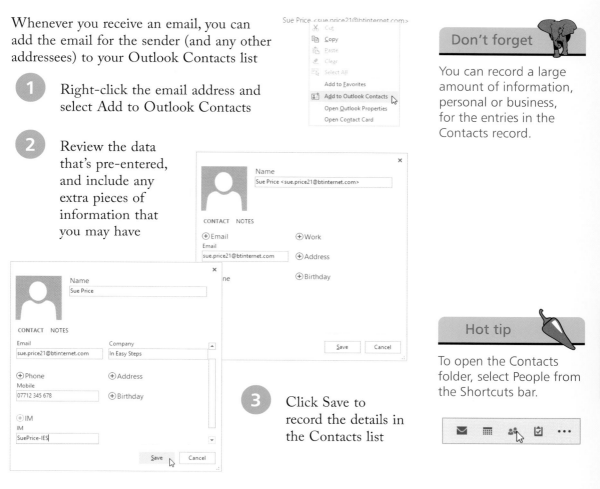

1 Right-click the email address and select Add to Outlook Contacts

2 Review the data that's pre-entered, and include any extra pieces of information that you may have

3 Click Save to record the details in the Contacts list

4 Open the Contacts folder to create and update entries

157

Don't forget

You can record a large amount of information, personal or business, for the entries in the Contacts record.

Hot tip

To open the Contacts folder, select People from the Shortcuts bar.

Don't forget

Double-click an entry to open it and review or amend the details. You can record a large amount of information, personal or business, for the entries in your Contacts folder.

Spam and Phishing

As useful as email can be, it does have problem areas. Because it is so cheap and easy to use, the criminally inclined take advantage of email for their own profit. They send out thousands of spam (junk email) messages, in the hope of getting one or two replies.

Beware

Don't respond in any way to messages that you think may be spam. Even clicking on an Unsubscribe link will confirm that your address is a genuine email account, and this may get it added to lists of validated account names.

Hot tip

Any message sent to the Junk Email folder is converted to plain-text format, and all links are disabled. In addition, the Reply and Reply All functions are disabled.

> ℹ️ Links and other functionality have been disabled in this message. To turn on that functionality, move this message to the Inbox.

The Outlook Junk Email filter identifies spam as messages are received, and moves the invalid messages to the Junk Email folder. To adjust the settings:

1 From the Home tab, select the Junk button in the Delete group, then click Junk Email Options...

2 Select your desired level of protection: No Automatic Filtering, Low (default), High or Safe Lists Only

3 Click the appropriate tab, to specify lists of safe senders, safe recipients or blocked senders and international domains

Don't forget

You can block messages from specified top level domain codes, and messages in particular foreign languages.

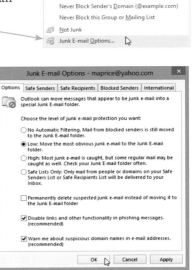

Outlook also provides protection from messages in the Inbox:

1 Links to pictures on the sender's website may be blocked, links to websites may be disabled, and you may not be allowed to use the Reply and Reply All functions

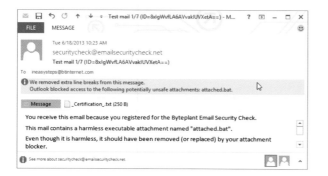

Hot tip

Links to pictures and other content from a website may be blocked, since these are sometimes the source of viruses and other threats. Only download them if you trust the sender.

If you want to explore how Outlook handles potentially damaging messages, visit website **www.emailsecuritycheck.net/**. Submit an email address, and respond to the confirming email.

Review the subsequent emails you receive from this website to see how Outlook responds to the various scenarios.

For example, Outlook blocks access to an attachment that's executable and so potentially dangerous.

Beware

Some spam messages and websites try to trick you into providing passwords, PINs, and personal details. Referred to as phishing (pronounced fishing),they appear to be from well-known organizations, such as banks, credit cards, and charities.

Don't forget

The attachments and links in these test emails are innocuous, but do illustrate ways in which the security of your system could be impacted.

Create a Message

Hot tip

You can also select New Email message from the Jump list, which appears when you right-click the program entry on the taskbar (or click the program entry pinned to the Start menu).

Don't forget

You can send the same message to more than one addressee. You can also select addressees for the Cc (courtesy copy) or Bcc (blind courtesy copy) options.

1 Select the Mail folder, and then click the New button to open a new mail message form

2 Click the To button to open the address book and list your contacts

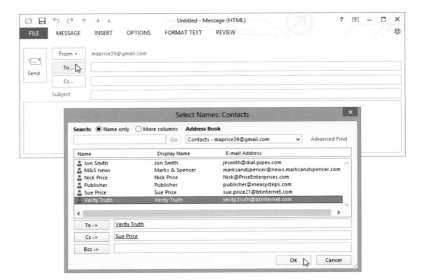

3 Select the addressee and click To, then add any other addressees and then click OK

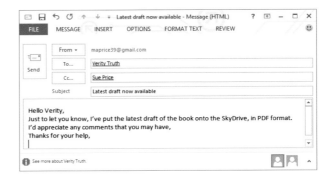

4 Type the subject, greeting, and text for your message

Insert a Signature

You can create a standard signature, to add to the emails you send.

1 Select the Insert tab and click Signature in the Include group, then click Signatures

2 Click the New button, specify a name for the new signature, then click OK

Hot tip

The first time you select the Signature button, there'll be no signatures defined, so you must start off by creating one.

Don't forget

You can specify one of your signatures as the default for new messages, or for replies and forwards, and the appropriate signature will be automatically applied for future messages.

161

3 Add the text required, and click OK to save the signature

4 When you've added one or more, click Signature again and select a signature to insert into the message, at the typing cursor location

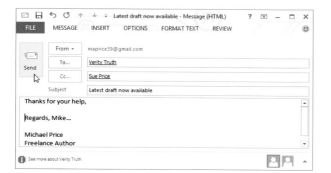

Don't forget

Click the Send button to store the message in the Outbox, ready for the next Send. Click the Send/ Receive tab and select Send/Receive to send immediately.

Message Tags

You can use tags to help sort and organize messages.

1 Select a message from a POP3 connection (see page 148) and select the Home tab

2 Click Unread/Read to toggle the read status of the selected message

HOME
Unread/ Read
Categorize ▾
Follow Up ▾

Unread/ Read

Hot tip

Email accounts that use an IMAP connection do not have the Categorize tag for their messages. Also, Follow Up is limited to a simple flag.

HOME
Unread/ Read
Follow Up ▾
Tags

Follow Up ▾
Flag Message
Clear Flag

3 Click Categorize to choose a color to associate with the selected message

HOME
Unread/ Read
Follow Up ▾
Tags

Rename Category

This is the first time you have used "Blue Category." Do you want to rename it?
Name: Blue Category
Color: [   ] ▾   Shortcut Key: (None) ▾
Yes   No

4 The first time you select a specific color, you'll be asked if you want to rename it, or assign it a shortcut key

5 The Categories column is added to the message details, and this field can also be used to group the messages

Don't forget

Choose Set Quick Click, to define the color category to be assigned when you single-click the Categories column.

Inbox - ineasysteps@btinternet.com - Outlook

FILE HOME SEND / RECEIVE FOLDER VIEW

New Email

All Unread Search Current Mailbox (Ctrl+E)   Current Mailbox ▾

Drag Your Favorite Folders Here

▲ ineasysteps@btinternet.com

!	☆	▯	⬚	FROM	SUBJECT	RECEIVED	CATEGORIES	SIZE	▽

▲ Date: Yesterday

Inbox 4
Sent Items
Deleted Items
Junk E-mail
Outbox

	Windows IT Pro	Messaging Related Reso...	Wed 6/19/2...	Blue Category	28 KB	⚑
	Windows Secrets	Avoiding those unwant...	Wed 6/19/2...	Red Category	179 KB	⚑
	Windows Secrets	Avoiding those unwant...	Wed 6/19/2...	Red Category	329 KB	⚑
	Windows Secrets	Welcome to the Windo...	Wed 6/19/2...	Red Category	20 KB	⚑

▲ Date: Tuesday

	securitycheck@em...	Test mail 4/7 (ID=8xIgWv...	Tue 6/18/20...	Yellow Category	10 KB	⚑
	securitycheck@em...	Test mail 6/7 (ID=8xIgWv...	Tue 6/18/20...	Yellow Category	10 KB	⚑
	securitycheck@em...	Test mail 7/7 (ID=8xIgWv...	Tue 6/18/20...	Yellow Category	10 KB	⚑
	securitycheck@em...	Test mail 5/7 (ID=8xIgWv...	Tue 6/18/20...	Yellow Category	10 KB	⚑

ITEMS: 13 UNREAD: 4   100%

Hot tip

You can select from a variety of predefined reminder notes.

Call
Do not Forward
Follow up
For Your Information
Forward
No Response Necessary
Read
Reply
Reply to All
Review

6 Click Follow Up to assign a flag to the selected message

Follow Up ▾
Today
Tomorrow
This Week
Next Week
No Date
Custom...
Add Reminder...
✓ Mark Complete
Clear Flag
Set Quick Click...

7 Select the appropriate flag, or add a To-Do item as a reminder

RSS Feeds

RSS (Really Simple Syndication) is a way for publishers of Internet data to make news, blogs, and other information available to subscribers. You can add feeds and view subscriptions in either Internet Explorer or Outlook.

To synchronize these programs:

1 Identify an RSS feed on a website by one of these active icons on the Command bar

2 Click the down arrow next to the icon and select one of the feeds offered

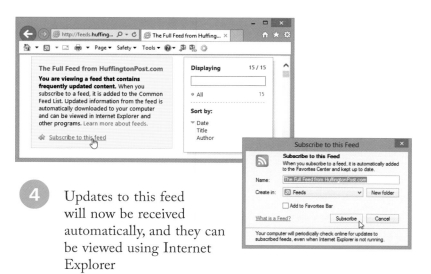

3 Click Subscribe to this feed, then click the Subscribe button to confirm

4 Updates to this feed will now be received automatically, and they can be viewed using Internet Explorer

Hot tip

Subscribing to RSS feeds from Internet Explorer is the quickest and easiest way to add RSS feeds to Outlook.

Hot tip

The RSS feeds you subscribe to using Internet Explorer are added to the Common Feed List and so can also be viewed using Outlook (see page 164).

You've successfully subscribed to this feed!
Updated content can be viewed in Internet Explorer and other programs that use the Common Feed List.

⭐ View my feeds

...cont'd

Hot tip

When you subscribe to RSS feeds from Internet Explorer, you can use Outlook to view the updates as they arrive.

To synchronize the RSS feeds and subscriptions in Outlook with those in Internet Explorer:

1 Click File, Open & Import, Import/Export, then select RSS Feeds from the Common Feed List, and click Next

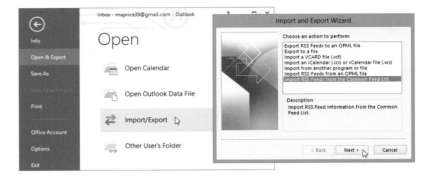

2 Select individual feeds to add to Outlook (or click the Select All button) and click Next, and then Finish

Don't forget

To ensure that the programs remain synchronized, select File, Options, Advanced, and then Synchronize RSS Feeds.

3 Select RSS Feeds in the Folders pane to view the updates

9 Time Management

Outlook is much more than an email manager. It is a complete personal information management system, with full diary and calendar facilities. It enables you to keep track of appointments and meetings, and to control and schedule your tasks. You can keep notes, make journal entries, and correlate all these with email messages relating to those records.

Outlook Calendar

The Outlook Calendar handles time-based activities, including appointments, meetings, holidays, courses, and events (single-day or multi-day). It provides a high-level view by day, week, or month and will give you reminders when an activity is due. To open:

 Click the Calendar button on the Navigation bar

Hot tip

To replace folder names by their associated icons, click the ••• dots and then Navigation Options.

Navigation Options...

Notes

Folders

Shortcuts

Navigation Options

Maximum number of visible items: 4

☑ Compact Navigation

Display in this order

Mail
Calendar
People
Tasks
Notes
Folders
Shortcuts

Move Up

Move Down

Reset   OK   Cancel

Adjust the number of items displayed and their display sequence, then click in the box for Compact Navigation.

Date navigator   Time bar   View   Events   Meeting

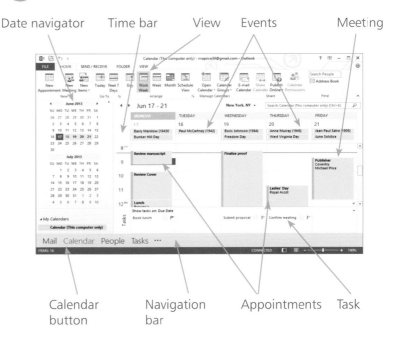

Calendar button   Navigation bar   Appointments   Task

You can also view current calendar events on the Today page:

 Click the Mail icon and select your email account

Don't forget

The Outlook Today page displays a summary of the calendar activities, the tasks, and the counts of unread messages on your system. Click the Calendar header to display the full calendar.

Schedule an Appointment

An appointment reserves space in your calendar for an activity that does not involve inviting other people, or for reserving resources.

1 Open the Calendar (day, week, or month view) and use the date navigator to select the day for the appointment

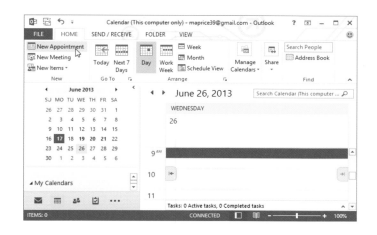

2 Using the mouse pointer select the time the appointment should begin, then click the New Appointment button

3 Type the subject, then select the end time, enter any other details you have, such as Location and Description, then select the Save & Close button

Hot tip

You can also double-click the Start time area, or right-click the area and select New Appointment.

Don't forget

To change the End time and duration, click the down-arrow and select a new value. You can also change the Start time (the current duration will be maintained).

Change Appointment Details

The appointment is added to the calendar, which shows the subject, start time, duration and location. Move the mouse over the appointment area to see more details.

Don't forget

Single-click the calendar at the appointment area and you can edit the text of the subject title. Double-click the area and you will open the appointment for edit.

① Select the appointment and the Calendar Tools tab is added, with related options displayed on the Ribbon

Hot tip

By default, you will get a reminder popup for the appointment 15 minutes before the start time, or you can set your own notice period (values between zero and two weeks), or turn off the reminder.

② Click Open (or double-click the appointment) to open the appointment editor form (see page 167), add or change any of the details (and then click Save & Close)

③ To change the start or finish times move the mouse pointer to the top or bottom edge and drag it to the required time. The duration changes to match

Recurring Appointments

When you have an activity that's repeated on a regular basis, you can define it as a recurring appointment.

 1 Open the appointments form and specify the details for a first occurrence of the activity, then click Recurrence

2 Specify how often the activity will be repeated, and over what range of time it should take place

3 Click OK, and then click Save & Close to record the changes

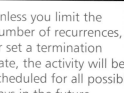

4 All the occurrences will be displayed in the calendar

Hot tip

You can take an existing appointment, or meeting, and click Recurrence to make it a recurring activity.

Beware

Unless you limit the number of recurrences, or set a termination date, the activity will be scheduled for all possible days in the future.

169

Don't forget

Depending on the view chosen and the space available, the recurrence symbol may appear after the subject in each entry.

Create a Meeting

Hot tip

You can convert an existing appointment into a meeting, by defining the attendees and sending invitations.

1 Double-click the appointment entry in the calendar, and click the Invite Attendees button in the Attendees group

2 On the invitation message form displayed, click the To button to open the contacts address list

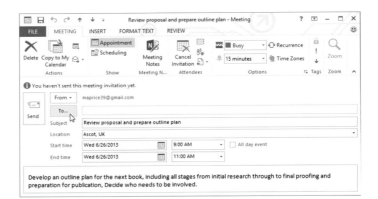

Don't forget

You can also schedule meeting resources, such as rooms, screens, and projectors.

3 Select the email address for each attendee in turn, and click Required or Optional as appropriate. Click OK when you've added all attendees

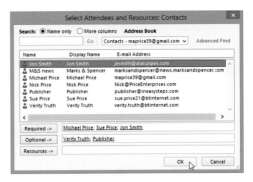

4 When all the attendees have been added, click the Send button to send the invitation to each of them

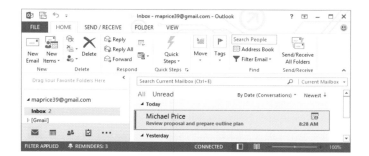

5 The invitation will be received in the organizer's Inbox

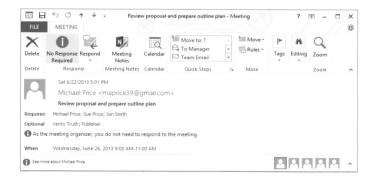

Don't forget

You can double-click the meeting entry in your calendar to view the current status, which will initially show No responses have been received for this meeting.

6 There's No Response Required from the organizer

Respond to an Invitation

172

Beware

The attendees must be using a version of Outlook in order to be able to properly receive and respond to meeting invitations.

1 When other attendees receive and open the invitation, it provides buttons to accept, decline, or to propose a new time

Hot tip

You can click the Tentative button to accept provisionally.

2 Click Accept, then select Send the Response Now, to add the appointment to your calendar

3 The original message is removed from the Inbox, and the response is inserted into the Sent box

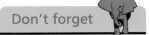
Don't forget

You can edit the response, if desired, or you can accept the invitation without sending a response. It will simply be added to your calendar.

4 The originator receives responses from attendees, as emails

Don't forget

The message shows the current status, so it will show the latest information each time it is opened.

5 The message shows the attendee's response and status

6 The meeting record displays the updated status

Hot tip

Any changes that the originator makes to the meeting details will be sent to the attendees as update messages.

Add Holidays

Hot tip

By default, no holidays or special events are shown in your Calendar, but Outlook does have a holiday file, with information for 112 countries and events for the years 2012–2022.

To make sure that your calendar is an accurate reflection of your availability, add details of national holidays and similar events.

1 Open Outlook, select File and then Options

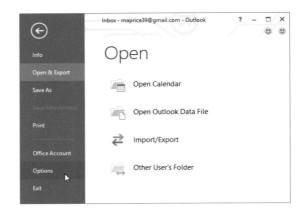

2 In Outlook Options, select Calendar then click the Add Holidays button in the Calendar options

Don't forget

Your own country or region is automatically selected each time you choose the Add Holidays option.

3 Select the country or countries that you wish to add, for example the United Kingdom and the United States, then click OK

4 The entries for the selected countries are imported

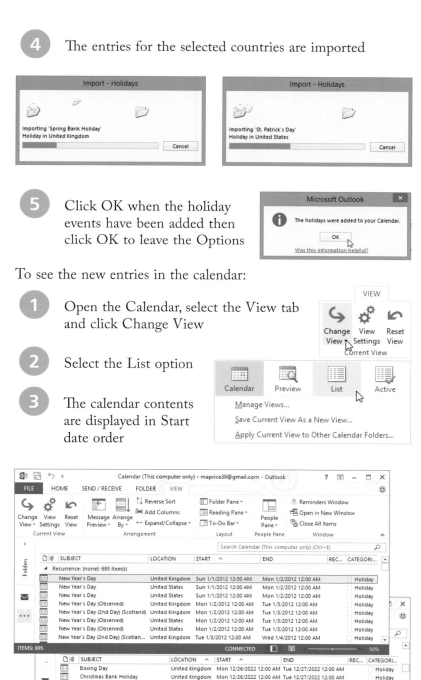

Don't forget

Your own country or region is automatically selected each time you choose the Add Holidays option.

5 Click OK when the holiday events have been added then click OK to leave the Options

To see the new entries in the calendar:

1 Open the Calendar, select the View tab and click Change View

2 Select the List option

3 The calendar contents are displayed in Start date order

175

Hot tip

If you have more than one country inserted, you can click Location to Group By This Field. Use this, for example, to remove the events for one country.

Report Free/Busy Time

Outlook can help you choose the most suitable times to hold meetings, based on reports from the proposed attendees, giving details of their availability.

To set up a procedure for publishing this information, each potential attendee should:

Hot tip

Sharing free/busy information works best on systems that use a Microsoft Exchange email server. For other systems, you may need to Import busy information (see page 177).

1 Open Outlook and select File, Options, Calendar

2 Click the Free/Busy Options button in Calendar Options

Don't forget

You could also set up a calendars and free/busy reports to coordinate the use of resources such as conference rooms and projector equipment.

3 Click the box for Publish at location, and provide the address for a networked folder or drive that is accessible by all potential attendees, then click OK

The free/busy data for the specified period (e.g. 2 months) and will be updated regularly (e.g. every 15 minutes). It will be stored at the location defined, in the form of username.vbf files (using the username from the attendee's email address).

Schedule a Meeting

You can use the reported free/busy information to help set up a meeting. For example, to schedule a new meeting:

 1 Create the meeting (see page 170) with initial details, such as expected start, duration, and proposed attendees

2 Click Scheduling, to show free/busy times, and click AutoPick Next to see the next available time slot

3 Click Send to add the revised details to your calendar, and to send an invitation (or an update) to all the attendees

Hot tip

You can use Scheduling to set up a new meeting, or to revise the timing for an existing meeting.

Beware

Free/Busy reports may not be available on your system or for particular attendees. In such cases, attendees can use select File, Save Calendar to save busy times.

You can then select File, Open & Export and then Import/Export to import their saved calendars and add their busy times to your calendar, ready to schedule the meeting.

177

Creating Tasks

Hot tip

Outlook can create and manage implicit tasks (as follow-ups of other Outlook items). It can also create explicit tasks, which can be assigned to others. To display the Task folder, click the ••• dots on the Navigation bar and select Tasks.

To create an implicit task:

1 Right-click an Outlook item (for example, a message or contact), select Follow Up and select the flag for the timing

2 The follow-up item is added to the Task folder, and also appears on the To-Do bar

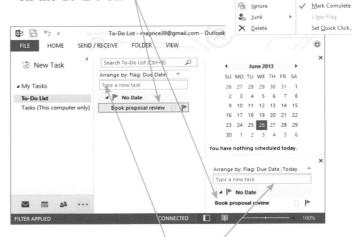

To create an explicit task:

1 Click the prompt "Type a new task" in the Task folder, or on the To-Do bar

2 Type the subject for the task, and then press Enter

3 The task is inserted into the Tasks folder, with the default characteristics (current date for the start date and the due date, and with no reminder time set)

Don't forget

This provides a quick way to generate a To-Do list of actions. Note that an entry changes color, to red, when its due date has passed.

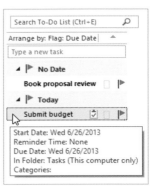

To make changes to the details for the task:

1 Double-click the task entry on the To-Do bar, or in the Task folder

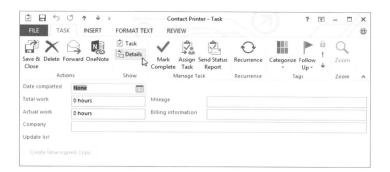

Don't forget

As with the editors for other Outlook items, the Task editor uses the Ribbon technology.

2 You can change the start date or the due date, add a description, apply a reminder, update the priority, or indicate how much has been completed

Hot tip

Click the arrows on the % Complete box to increase or decrease by 25% at a time, or type an exact percentage in the box.

3 When you update the % Complete, the status changes to In progress or Complete, or you can click the down-arrow to choose an alternative status value

4 Click the Details button in the Show group to add information about carrying out the task, e.g. hours worked

Don't forget

Click Save & Close, in Task or Details view, to record the changes.

Assigning Tasks

You can define a task that someone else is to perform, assign it to that person and get status reports and updates on its progress.

To assign an existing task:

Hot tip

To create and assign a new task, select New and Task Request from the menu bar, or press Ctrl + Shift + U. Then enter the subject and other task details, along with the assignee name.

1 Open the task and click the Assign Task button, in Manage Task

Don't forget

Select or clear the boxes for Keep an updated copy of this task on my task list and Send me a status report when this task is complete, as desired.

2 In the To box, type the name or email address for the assignee, or click the To button and select an entry from the Contacts list

3 Click Send, to initiate the task-assignment request, then click OK to confirm the new ownership

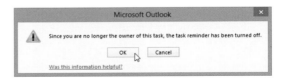

4 The message will be sent to the assignee, with a copy stored in the Sent Items folder

180

Accepting Task Requests

1 The task details on the originating system shows that it is awaiting a response from the recipient of the task request

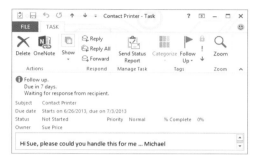

2 The task request appears in the recipient's Inbox

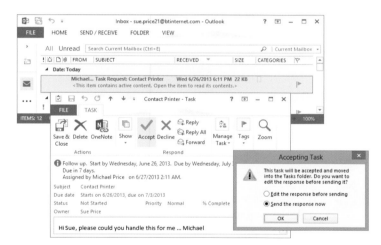

If the task is rejected, ownership is returned to the originator, who can then assign the task to another person.

181

3 The recipient opens the message, clicks the Accept button, then clicks OK to send the response

The task request is sent to the originator, and a copy is saved in the Sent Items folder.

Confirming the Assignment

1 The response appears in the originator's Inbox, as a message from the recipient of the task request

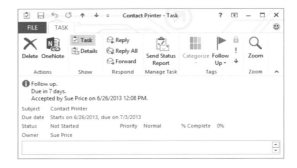

2 When the message is opened, it shows the task with its change of ownership

Don't forget

The originator is no longer able to make changes to the task details, since ownership has been transferred to the recipient.

3 The task appears in the originator's Tasks folder, grouped under the new owner's name

4 The new owner can change task details, and click Save & Close to save them, as the task progresses

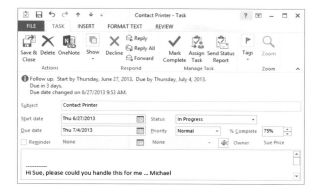

Hot tip

When the recipient makes any changes to the task details, messages are sent to the originator, to update the entry in the task folder.

5 For each change, the originator is sent an update message, to change the details of the task in the task folder

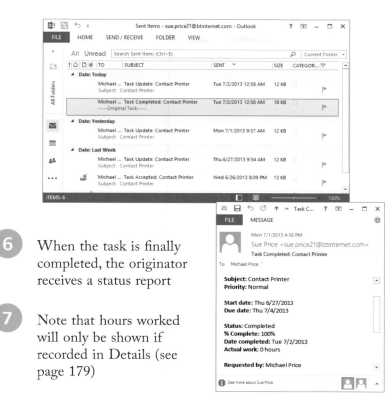

6 When the task is finally completed, the originator receives a status report

7 Note that hours worked will only be shown if recorded in Details (see page 179)

Don't forget

Click the message box to list all related messages, in the Inbox or Sent Items folders.

Notes

You may need a prompt, but the activity doesn't justify creating a task or an appointment. In such a case, you can use Outlook Notes. To create a note from anywhere in Outlook:

Hot tip

Outlook Notes are the electronic equivalent of sticky notes, and they can be used for anything you need to remember.

1 Press shortcut key Ctrl + Shift + N

2 Type the text for your note in the form that's displayed, and it will be added to the Notes folder

Remember the Windows 8.1 preview is being released today. Check for download at windows.microsoft.com/en-us/windows-8/preview

6/26/2013 10:23 AM

3 Click the ⋯ dots on the Navigation bar and select Notes to see the current set of notes stored in that folder

Don't forget

You can leave the note open, or click the [X] Close button. In either case, there's no need to save the note – it is recorded automatically.

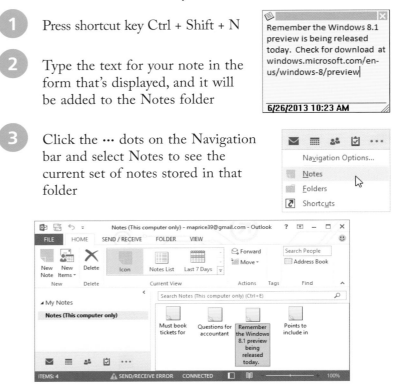

4 The note titles may be truncated, so select a note to see its full title – the text up to the first Enter, or else the whole text, if there's no Enter symbol

5 Select the View tab and click List (or Small Icons) to allow more space for the note titles

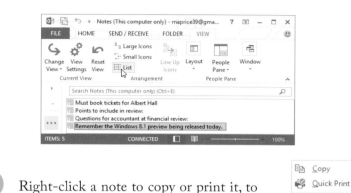

Don't forget

The notes are of a standard size, but you can click and drag an edge or a corner to make a note any size you wish.

6 Right-click a note to copy or print it, to forward it to another user, or to delete it

To change the settings for the Current View of your Notes folder:

185

1 Select the View tab then click View Settings to adjust Sort or Filter options

Hot tip

The settings for the Icon view are shown. There'll be a different set of options available if you choose the Notes List or the Last 7 Days views.

2 Click Other Settings to adjust the options that manage the icon placement

Journal

You can record information about activities related to Outlook items in the Journal, a type of project log book.

Beware

In previous versions Journal recorded activities automatically. In Outlook 2013 you enter items manually. Journal is being reduced in function, so you should consider alternative methods for managing activities, for example, using Tasks.

Don't forget

You can select from a wide variety of Journal entry types.

Conversation
Document
E-mail Message
Fax
Letter
Meeting
Meeting cancellation
Meeting request
Meeting response
Microsoft Excel
Microsoft Office Access
Microsoft PowerPoint
Microsoft Word
Note
Phone call
Remote session
Task
Task request
Task response

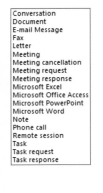

Hot tip

You can drag & drop items from Mail, Calendar and other Outlook folders to add them to the Journal.

1 Click the ··· dots on the Navigation bar and select Folders, then select Journal from the Folders pane

2 Alternatively, press shortcut key Ctrl + 8 to open the Journal directly

3 Select Journal Entry to create a new item

4 Enter details then click Save & Close

5 Entries are displayed on a Timeline

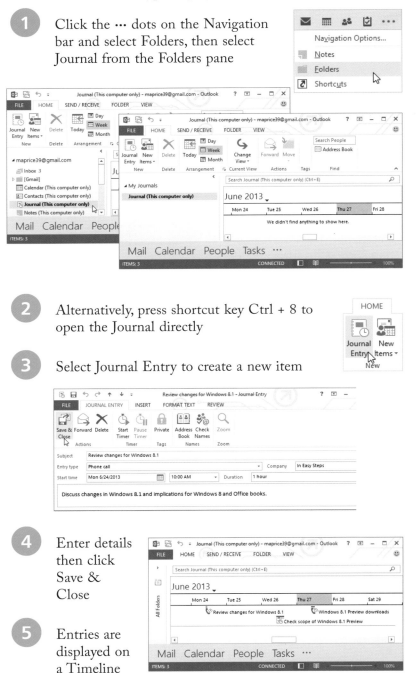

10 Manage Files and Fonts

It is useful to understand how Office stores and manages the files that constitute the documents and the fonts they use, so that you can choose the appropriate formats when you share documents with other users across the Internet.

Windows Version

Although most features of Office 2013 are independent of the actual version of Windows you are using, there are differences to watch out for, when starting any of the Office applications and managing the associated files and folders.

To illustrate the differences:

1 In **Windows 7**, select Start, More Programs then double-click Microsoft Office 2013

2 Select Word 2013 from the Office 2013 folder

3 From Word 2013 select File and then click Open

4 Choose the file location, for example select Computer, My Documents to access your Documents library then choose a document, e.g. Overview

These screenshots show the use of the Start menu to open applications, and also illustrate the use of the Windows 7 Aero Glass theme, which provides animation and transparency effects (where supported by the hardware and Windows 7 edition).

Hot tip

Despite the switch from Start menu to Start screen and contrasts in style between Windows 7 and Windows 8, most operations in Office 2013 will be the same. However, there are some differences in the ways that you manage files.

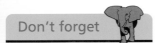

Don't forget

If your system uses the Home Basic edition of Windows 7, this is functionally the same, but does not display the Aero Glass transparency effects.

1 In **Windows 8**, display the Start screen and select the Word 2013 tile

2 Alternatively, select Desktop from the Start screen and click the Word 2013 shortcut on the Taskbar

Don't forget

If the Taskbar does not show a shortcut for a particular application, you can right-click its tile on the Start screen and select Pin to Taskbar.

3 From Word 2013 select File and then click Open

4 Choose the file location and location the document that you want to open, e.g. My Documents and Overview

This shows ways in which you open applications in Windows 8.

There is no Aero Glass effect in this version of Windows, but the contents of the windows and the functions offered are just the same as those provided in the Windows 7 environment.

In both cases, the option is offered to Search Documents, to help you locate documents by name or by content.

Hot tip

When you select My Documents, you access the Documents library for the current user, just as in Windows 7, but the File Explorer window does not choose to highlight this aspect.

Library Location

To see where on your system your library of documents is located:

1 In the Open window, select the Documents library in the Navigation pane and click the triangle to expand it (or simply double-click Documents to expand the library)

Hot tip

Right-click one of the documents and select Open File Location, to switch to the specific folder containing your documents.

2 Select the My Documents location that's displayed and you'll see it has the documents shown in the library

3 Click the address area and it will be converted into drive address format, showing that the user's documents are in the folder C:\Users\username\documents

Don't forget

You'll see the same results for the Windows 7 version. This also stores your documents in folder username\documents.

C:\Users\Michael\Documents ▾ ↩

Finding Files

The search facilities are one of the strengths of Windows 7 or 8, and Office 2013 takes full advantage of them. To illustrate this, suppose you've created a document discussing the Stayman bridge convention, but appear to have saved it in the wrong folder.

To track it down, when using Office 2013 with Windows 8:

 1 Open Word 2013 and select File, Open, then choose the starting location for example Computer, My Documents

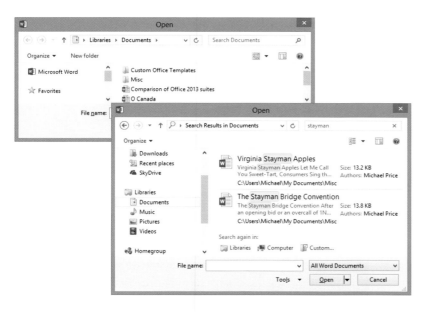

Hot tip

Select Documents, or choose another folder or drive where you expect to find your missing document.

2 Click in the Search box, and type the search terms, for example, Stayman. Matching documents from the starting location and its subfolders are displayed immediately

3 Select the Content view to see details of the files, including parts of the text and the full path

4 Right-click a file, and select Open file location, to see the folder where it is stored. Double-click the file to open it in Word and view or edit its contents

Don't forget

This shows that the required document has been misfiled in the Misc folder within Documents. You'll get similar results using Windows 7.

Beware

Any documents that contain the specified word in their titles, or in their contents, will be selected.

191

| Extra large icons |
| Large icons |
| Medium icons |
| Small icons |
| List |
| Details |
| Tiles |
| Content |

...cont'd

Don't forget

Although Word is used in these examples, the same search procedures apply for documents in other Office applications, for example, Excel and PowerPoint.

To locate documents using the operating system Search facility:

1 In Windows 7, click the Start button and simply type the search term, e.g. stayman

2 Matching documents, applications and other files are identified and listed so you can locate or open them

Don't forget

Hold the mouse pointer over a search result, and the tooltip will show the location where the file or document is stored.

3 In Windows 8, display the Start screen and again simply type the search term to automatically invoke Search

4 Windows 8 counts matches for Apps, Settings and Files, but lists only the Apps. Click another category if needed

Recent Documents

When you want to return to a document that you worked with previously, you may find it in the list of recently-used documents.

1 Select File, Open and click Recent Documents and click an entry in the Recent Documents list to open it

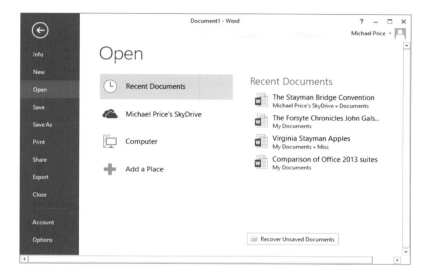

2 You can also right-click the application icon on the Taskbar to display the Jump list which shows Recent items

Windows 7

In Windows 7, you can select an application on the Start menu to see a list of its recent items.

The Start menu may also offer the Recent Items entry which will list recently-used files for a number of different applications, for example Word, Excel and PowerPoint.

Beware

If a document is moved or renamed, the entry in Recent Documents is not updated, so it will give an error indicating Document not found.

193

Hot tip

Right-click on an unwanted item, and select Remove from list. Choose Clear unpinned Documents, to remove all the items.

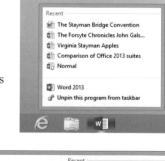

Change File Type

To change the file types listed when you open documents:

1 From Word 2013, select the File tab, click Open and select the file location, e.g. My Documents\Misc

Hot tip

Showing additional file types will make it easier to locate the correct document, when you use a variety of file types in your applications.

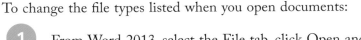

2 Choose the file type or group of types, All Word Documents, for example

3 Files of the specified type are listed

Don't forget

You can have more than one document with the same name, but different file extensions, if you have, for example, Office 2013 and Office 2003 versions.

4 You must change folder views in File Explorer (see page 22) to show file name extensions for the documents

XML File Formats

Office 2013 uses file formats based on XML, first introduced in Office 2007. They apply to Word 2013, Excel 2013, PowerPoint 2013 and Visio 2013. The XML file types include:

Application	XML file type	Extension
Word	Document	.docx
	Macro-enabled document	.docm
	Template	.dotx
	Macro-enabled template	.dotm
Excel	Workbook	.xlsx
	Macro-enabled workbook	.xlsm
	Template	.xltx
	Macro-enabled template	.xltm
	Non-XML binary workbook	.xlsb
	Macro-enabled add-in	.xlam
PowerPoint	Presentation	.pptx
	Macro-enabled presentation	.pptm
	Template	.potx
	Macro-enabled template	.potm
	Macro-enabled add-in	.ppam
	Show	.ppsx
	Macro-enabled show	.ppsm
Visio	Drawing	.vsdx
	Macro-enabled drawing	.vsdm
	Stencil	.vssx
	Macro-enabled stencil	.vssm
	Template	.vstx
	Macro-enabled template	.vstm

Don't forget

The .docx, .xlsx and .pptx file format extensions are also used for the Strict Open XML formats, which are ISO versions of the XML formats.

195

The XML formats are automatically compressed, and can be up to 75% smaller, saving disk space and reducing transmission sizes and times when you send files via email or across the Internet.

Files are structured in a modular fashion, which keeps different data components in the file separate from each other. This allows files to be opened, even if a component within the file (for example, a chart or table) is damaged or corrupted (see page 202).

Hot tip

This is all handled automatically. You do not have to install any special zip utilities to open and close files in Office 2013.

Save As PDF or XPS

There are times when you'd like to allow other users to view and print your documents, but you'd rather they didn't make changes. These could include résumés, legal documents, newsletters, or any other documents that are meant for review only. Office 2013 provides for this situation, with two built-in file formats.

Portable Document Format (PDF)

PDF is a fixed-layout file format that preserves your document formatting when the file is viewed online or printed, while the data in the file cannot be easily changed. The PDF format is also useful for documents that will be published, using commercial printing methods.

XML Paper Specification (XPS)

XPS also preserves document formatting and protects the data content. However, it is not yet widely used. The XPS format ensures that, when the file is viewed online or printed, it retains the exact format you intended, and that data in the file cannot be easily changed.

To save an Office document in either format:

1 Open the document in the appropriate application, for example, open a Word document using Word 2013

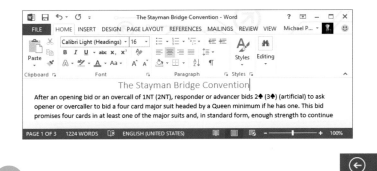

2 Make any required changes to the document, then select the File tab and click Save

3 Select the location to store the new copy. The default is the current folder, in this case in My Documents\Misc

Hot tip

PDF was developed, and is supported by, Adobe, which provides a free Reader for viewing and printing PDF files. XPS is a competitive product from Microsoft, who also provide a free XPS viewer.

Don't forget

All the Office 2013 applications include the capability to save documents or reports in the PDF and XPS formats.

4 Click the Save as type box, and select PDF or XPS format

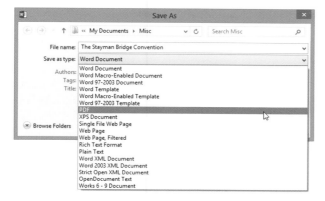

Hot tip

You can also save a copy of your document in one of the formats that are suitable for use on web pages, or in a variety of other formats.

5 Select Standard or Online quality, and then click Save

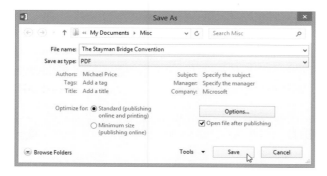

Don't forget

You can optimize the document for online viewing or for printing, and you can choose to open the file after it has been stored.

6 The document is saved to disk in the required format, and then displayed using the Microsoft Reader app, which supports both PDF and XPS formats

Fonts in Office 2013

There are a number of fonts provided with Office 2013, such as Calibri, Comic Sans, Gabriola, Georgia, Impact and Verdana. You can preview text using these and other Windows fonts:

1 From the Home tab, select the text to be previewed, click the down-arrow on the Font box

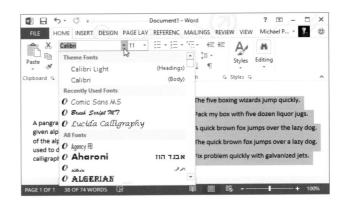

2 Scroll the list to locate an interesting font, then move the mouse pointer over the font name to see an immediate preview using that font

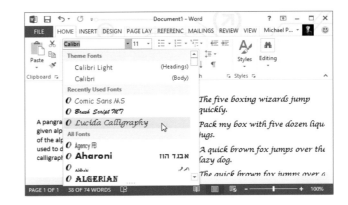

3 Click on the desired font name to put the change into effect

This helps indicate how the text will appear, but it is an awkward way to explore the large number of fonts available.

Hot tip

Calibri is the default font for Office 2013, replacing the Times New Roman font that was used in earlier versions of Office.

Beware

The font sample box usually extends over the text, hiding much of the preview. It can be dragged up to reveal more of the text, but will then display fewer fonts.

...cont'd

With the help of a macro available from Microsoft, you can create a document that provides a sample of every font on your system.

 1 Visit **support.microsoft.com/kb/209205**

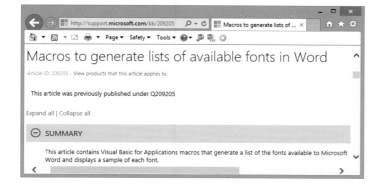

Hot tip

There are two macros. ListFonts creates a document with samples for each font. ListAllFonts provides similar content, but uses a table format.

2 Scroll down to ListAllFonts, and select the code

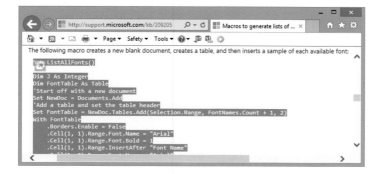

Don't forget

Highlight all the lines of code, ready for copying, from the first line:
    Sub ListAllFonts()
to the last line:
    End Sub

3 Open a new blank document, and select the View tab, ready to work with macros

Create and Run ListAllFonts

1 Click the arrow on the Macros button in the Macros group, and select the View Macros entry

Hot tip

Just clicking on the Macros button will select and carry out the View Macros action.

2 Name the macro ListAllFonts, choose Macros in Document1, and click Create

3 Highlight the skeleton code to replace it

```
Macros                                    ? ×
Macro name:
ListAllFonts
                                          Run
                                          Step Into
                                          Edit
                                          Create
                                          Delete
                                          Organizer...
Macros in:  Document1 (document)
Description:
                                          Cancel
```

```
Microsoft Visual Basic for Applications - Document1
File  Edit  View  Insert  Format  Debug  Run  Tools  Add-Ins  Window  Help
                                                            Ln 1, Col 1
Project - Project
  Normal
  Project (Document1)
    Microsoft Word Objects
    Modules
      NewMacros
    References

Document1 - NewMacros (Code)
(General)                    ListAllFonts
Sub ListAllFonts()

' ListAllFonts Macro

End Sub
```

```
Microsoft Visual Basic for Applications - Document1
File  Edit  View  Insert  Format  Debug  Run  Tools  Add-Ins  Window  Help
                                                            Ln 30, Col 8
Project - Project
  Normal
  Project (Document1)
    Microsoft Word Objects
    Modules
      NewMacros
    References

Properties - NewMacros
NewMacros Module
Alphabetic  Categorized
(Name) NewMacros

Document1 - NewMacros (Code)
(General)                    ListAllFonts
Sub ListAllFonts()

Dim J As Integer
Dim FontTable As Table
'Start off with a new document
Set NewDoc = Documents.Add
'Add a table and set the table header
Set FontTable = NewDoc.Tables.Add(Selection.Range, FontNames.Count + 1, 2)
With FontTable
    .Borders.Enable = False
    .Cell(1, 1).Range.Font.Name = "Arial"
    .Cell(1, 1).Range.Font.Bold = 1
    .Cell(1, 1).Range.InsertAfter "Font Name"
    .Cell(1, 2).Range.Font.Name = "Arial"
    .Cell(1, 2).Range.Font.Bold = 1
    .Cell(1, 2).Range.InsertAfter "Font Example"
End With
'Go through all the fonts and add them to the table
For J = 1 To FontNames.Count
    With FontTable
        .Cell(J + 1, 1).Range.Font.Name = "Arial"
        .Cell(J + 1, 1).Range.Font.Size = 10
        .Cell(J + 1, 1).Range.InsertAfter FontNames(J)
        .Cell(J + 1, 2).Range.Font.Name = FontNames(J)
        .Cell(J + 1, 2).Range.Font.Size = 10
        .Cell(J + 1, 2).Range.InsertAfter "ABCDEFG abcdefg 1234567890"
    End With
Next J
FontTable.Sort SortOrder:=wdSortOrderAscending
End Sub
```

Don't forget

This stores the macro in the current document, ready to run.

4 Copy and paste the code from the Microsoft website, then select File, Close and Return to Microsoft Word

```
File  Edit  View  Insert  Format  Debug  Run
  Save Document1                     Ctrl+S
  Import File...                     Ctrl+M
  Export File...                     Ctrl+E
  Remove NewMacros...
  Print...                           Ctrl+P
X Close and Return to Microsoft Word  Alt+Q
```

5 Reselect View Macros, click the macro name ListAllFonts, and then click Run

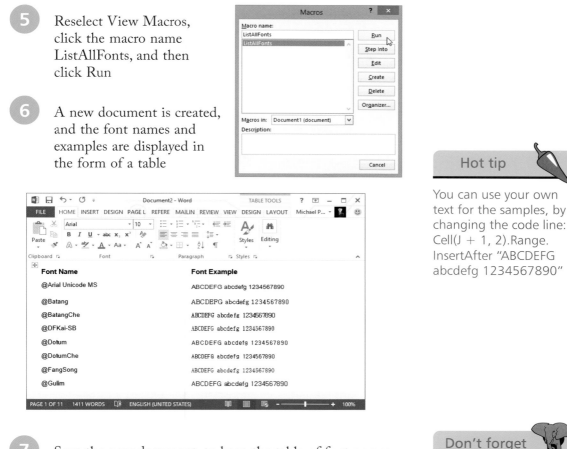

6 A new document is created, and the font names and examples are displayed in the form of a table

Font Name	Font Example
@Arial Unicode MS	ABCDEFG abcdefg 1234567890
@Batang	ABCDEFG abcdefg 1234567890
@BatangChe	ABCDEFG abcdefg 1234567890
@DFKai-SB	ABCDEFG abcdefg 1234567890
@Dotum	ABCDEFG abcdefg 1234567890
@DotumChe	ABCDEFG abcdefg 1234567890
@FangSong	ABCDEFG abcdefg 1234567890
@Gulim	ABCDEFG abcdefg 1234567890

Hot tip

You can use your own text for the samples, by changing the code line: Cell(J + 1, 2).Range. InsertAfter "ABCDEFG abcdefg 1234567890"

201

7 Save the new document, to keep the table of font names and examples for future reference. Save the first document to keep a copy of the ListAllFonts macro

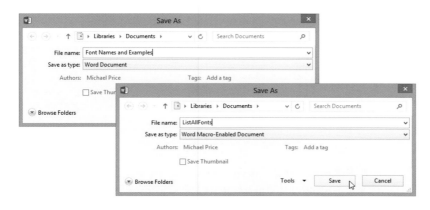

Don't forget

The macro is created in the first document, which can be closed without saving. It is not required to view the font samples in the second document. However, if you do want to save the original document, you must make it a macro-enabled document.

Document Recovery

Sometimes your system may, for one reason or another, close down before you have saved the changes to the document you were working on. The next time you start the application concerned, the Document Recovery feature will recover as much of the work you'd carried out as possible since you last saved it.

 Open the program (e.g. Word) and click Show Recovered Documents

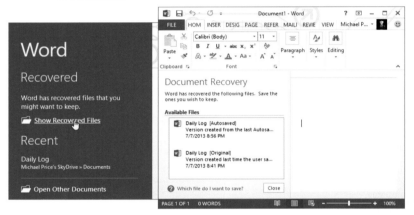

Don't forget

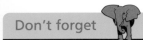

If a program freezes, you may have to force Logoff, or Shutdown without being able to save your document.

 Check the versions of the document that are offered, and choose the one closest to your requirements

 Select File, Save As, then rename and save the document

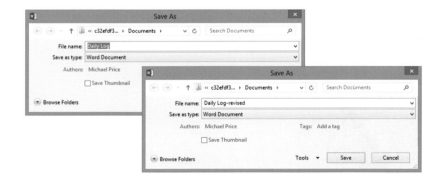

Don't forget

By default, documents are autosaved every ten minutes, but you can adjust the timing (see page 30).

Provide a different name for the autosaved version, "Daily Log-revised", for example, if you want to retain the original version also.

11 Up-to-Date and Secure

Microsoft Update makes sure that you take advantage of updates to Office. You can get the latest information and guidance, with the online help. Office also provides the options to enable you to protect your documents, control access to them and secure your system.

Enable Updates

Don't forget

After you install Office 2013 and run any of the applications for the first time, you will be asked to Activate your copy of Office and then choose the settings for Update.

1 The first time you run an Office 2013 application you'll be asked to choose your preferred settings for Update

First things first.   ×

● Use recommended settings
   Install important and recommended updates for Office, Windows and
   other Microsoft software and help improve Office.

○ Install updates only
   Install important and recommended updates for Office, Windows and
   other Microsoft software.

○ Ask me later
   Until you decide, your computer might be vulnerable to security threats.

The information sent to Microsoft is to help us and is not used to identify or
contact you.
We take your privacy seriously.
Learn more

                                                            Accept

The recommended settings will provide you with updates for Office, Windows, and other Microsoft software, together with various problem-solving facilities. Alternatively, you can choose to install updates only.

You can choose not to apply updates, though this can leave your computer open to security threats. However, you can change the update settings at a later date:

Hot tip

In Windows 7, select the Start button then click Control Panel on the Start menu. In Windows 8, switch to the Desktop, display the Charms bar, click Settings and then select Control Panel.

1 Open the Control Panel and select System and Security, then Windows Update

System and Security
Review your computer's status
Save backup copies of your files with File History
Find and fix problems

2 To initiate updates for Office 2013 and other Microsoft products, click Find out more

Windows Update
Turn automatic updating on or off
Check for updates
Install optional updates
View update history

3 The Windows Update web page opens. Agree the Terms of Use and click the Install button

Don't forget

There's a similar process for updating Office 2013, and other Microsoft software running under Windows 7.

4 Microsoft Update is installed and you are reminded how to search for Windows Update from the Start screen

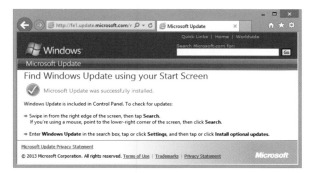

5 Windows Update checks for updates for Windows, Office and other products as defined by the revised settings

Hot tip

Windows Update will in future automatically check for updates, and will also automatically install them.

Apply Updates

 Windows Update shows you how many updates there are

 To see details, click the link showing the number found

Hot tip

You can select the View Update History link to see details of the updates that have been applied.

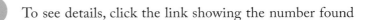

Windows Update will install the updates automatically, or you can click the Install button to install the updates immediately

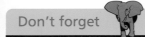

Don't forget

When updating has been completed, you may be prompted to restart the system to fully apply all the updates.

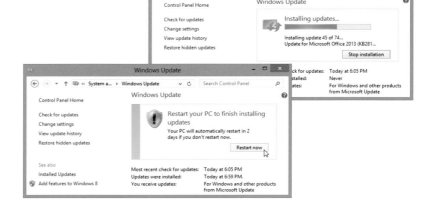

Change Settings

To view and change the settings for Windows Update:

 1 Open Windows Update from the Control Panel, or using the suggested search from the Start screen (see page 205)

Hot tip

In Windows 7, you can select Start, All Programs and find an entry for Windows Update on the Start menu.

2 Select Change Settings to view or change values

3 Review the details for the update action, including the time of day when scheduled maintenance is carried out

Don't forget

Windows Update will schedule updates daily at the specified time, as long as the computer is not otherwise busy.

Automatic Maintenance
Run maintenance tasks daily at 3:00 AM ▾

207

Office Help

There are two ways to display the Office Help for an application. With the application open:

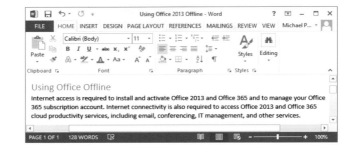

Hot tip

You invoke Office Help in the same way in each Office application, though the Help window that opens is specific to the active application, in this case, Word. The layout is similar for all the Office applications.

1   Press the F1 shortcut on the keyboard

2   Click the **?** icon at the right of the titlebar

You'll see a variety of useful items all related to the Word application. Open the Help window from Excel, and you will see similar items, but tailored specifically to Excel.

If your computer is offline, only the Basic Office help is offered.

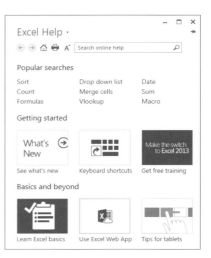

Don't forget

To get the full content for Help topics, you must have an internet connection. Otherwise you'll have only Offline help which offers very basic information (see page 210).

Explore Help Topics

 Enter keywords for a search topic, or select one of the Popular searches, for example, Word count

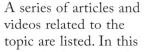

 A series of articles and videos related to the topic are listed. In this example there are 15 articles and 7 videos

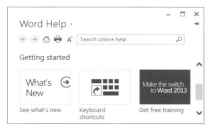

3 The Getting Started section has links to a video and article on new features in Word 2013, an article on Keyboard Shortcuts and a series of training videos

4 The Basics and beyond section introduces basic tasks in Word and in the Word Web App, plus Tips for tablets, a link to the Office Touch Guide

Hot tip

Unlike previous versions of Microsoft Office, the Help offered is not context sensitive, so you always start with the same selection of items.

Don't forget

Whichever topic you select, you will still have the Search box so you can locate new topics, or click the Home button to return to the initial Help window.

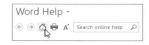

Offline Help

1 If you have no Internet connection when you select Office Help, you'll be offered limited Offline Basic Help

Hot tip

The change to Offline status will be applied to all Office applications, and will be retained until explicitly changed.

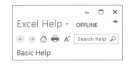

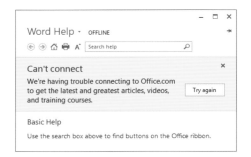

2 To see the Offline Help even with a connection, click the arrow next to Help and select Help from your computer

Beware

You will find yourself limited to basic help while flying, when you are using your computer in Airplane mode.

3 Enter a search term, e.g. print, and press Enter to get basic information about Print buttons on the Ribbon

4 Click the result to get any extra details, such as the shortcut keys

Developer Tab

The Developer tab provides access to functions that are useful if you want to create or run macros or develop applications to use with Office programs. It is aimed at the advanced user and for this reason, it is normally hidden.

To reveal the Developer tab in a particular Office application:

1 Open the application and select the File tab, then click Options

2 In the Options for that application, select Customize Ribbon

Don't forget

Enabling the Developer tab for one Office application does not enable it in any of the other applications. You must enable (or disable) the Developer tab for each application individually.

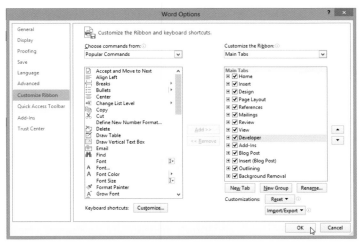

Hot tip

The selection of groups included in the Developer tab vary by application. For example, Word has the 6 shown, Excel has 5 and PowerPoint has 4.

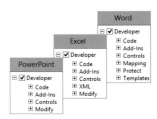

3 Click the Developer box, which is initially unticked, and then click OK, and the Developer tab is added

Remove Personal Information

There can be more in the file version of an Office document than the information that appears when you review or print it. If the document has been subject to revision, there could be a record of all the changes, including original or deleted text and data. Any comments that reviewers may have added could still be there.

Hot tip

The markup includes all the changes and comments that have been applied, and may give away more information than you'd really like.

1 Select the Review tab, and click the No Markup button

2 Select All Markup and you'll see that the file contains the original text, as well changes and comments

If you share online copies of the document, you may not want such information included. Office 2013 makes it easy to completely remove such information from the published versions of the document.

Beware

Do not make changes to your master document. It is best to work with a copy of the document, to avoid the possibility of accidentally removing too much information.

3 Select File, Save as, enter a new name for the document and click the Save button

4 Select the File tab, click Info, then click the Check for Issues button, and select Inspect Document

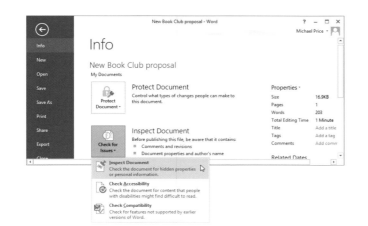

Don't forget

You can also check for accessibility issues and compatibility issues, before making your document available.

5 Click Remove All for each item in turn, where unwanted or unnecessary data was found

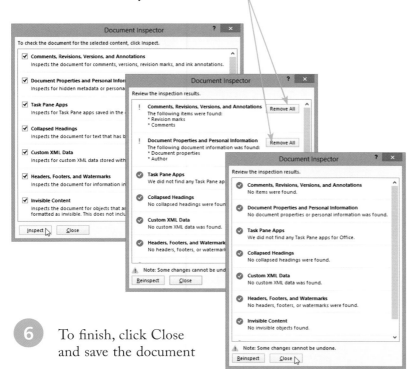

Hot tip

Select those elements that may contain hidden information that you want to remove. You might allow items, such as headers, footers and watermarks, if detected.

6 To finish, click Close and save the document

Don't forget

If you've used a working copy, the information will still be available in the original document, just in case it's needed.

Protect Your Documents

At the simplest level, you could tell users that the document has been completed, and should no longer be changed.

Don't forget

When you send out a document, you might want to discourage or prevent others from making unauthorized changes to the content.

 Open the document, select the File tab, click Info, and then Protect Document, and select Mark as Final

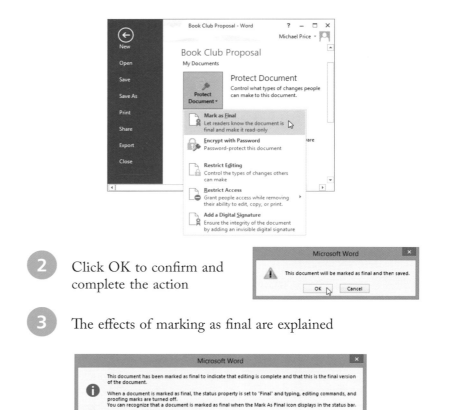

Don't forget

Another way to make the document read-only is to publish it using the PDF, or XPS document format (see page 196).

 Click OK to confirm and complete the action

 The effects of marking as final are explained

Hot tip

The Ribbon and all its commands are hidden, and the Info for the document confirms the new status.

 This is illustrated when you next open the document. You see Read-Only on the title bar, and a warning message

Alternatively, you might choose to encrypt the document, to prohibit unauthorized changes.

1 From Info, Protect Document, select Encrypt with Password

Beware

If you lose the password, the document cannot be recovered, so you should work with a copy, and retain the original document in secure storage.

2 Provide a password for the document, click OK, then re-enter the password to confirm, and click OK again

3 The contents haven't been altered, but when you close the document, you will still be prompted to save the changes

Don't forget

With encryption applied, no one will be able to review or change the document without the correct password, as will be indicated in the document Info.

4 Now, anyone who opens the document will be required to enter the password and click OK

If you want to remove the encryption:

5 Open the document (using the password) then select Encrypt Document, as above, delete the existing password and click OK

Restrict Permission

You can go further and apply specific levels of protection.

Don't forget

You can also click the Review tab and then the Restrict Editing button to display this pane.

When you have selected the styles that are allowed, you can choose to remove any existing formatting or styles that would now be disallowed.

Don't forget

You can give specific users permission to freely edit particular sections of the document.

Hot tip

1 Working with a copy of your document, click File, Info, Protect Document, and select Restrict Editing

2 The Restrict Formatting and Editing task pane appears

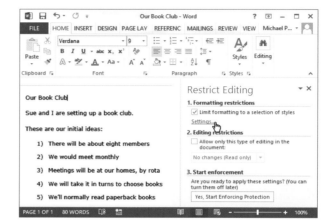

3 Choose the option to Limit formatting to a selection of styles, and click Settings, to say what styles you want in the document

4 Choose the option to Allow this type of editing in the document, and select the level you will allow

5 Click the button labeled Yes, Start Enforcing Protection

6 Choose the protection method. For home use, you should select Password (supplying a revised password if desired)

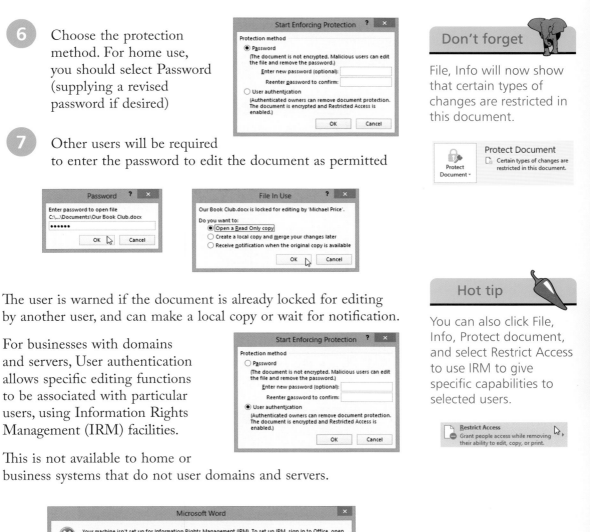

7 Other users will be required to enter the password to edit the document as permitted

The user is warned if the document is already locked for editing by another user, and can make a local copy or wait for notification.

For businesses with domains and servers, User authentication allows specific editing functions to be associated with particular users, using Information Rights Management (IRM) facilities.

This is not available to home or business systems that do not user domains and servers.

In previous versions of Office you could use IRM via a Microsoft account. If you have existing IRM protected documents, you can continue to use the service, even without server capabilities.

Finally, an invisible digital signature ensures document integrity.

8 From File, Info, Protect Document, select Add a Digital Signature

Don't forget

File, Info will now show that certain types of changes are restricted in this document.

Protect Document — Certain types of changes are restricted in this document.

Hot tip

You can also click File, Info, Protect document, and select Restrict Access to use IRM to give specific capabilities to selected users.

Restrict Access — Grant people access while removing their ability to edit, copy, or print.

Don't forget

You'll need to obtain a digital ID from one of the suppliers at the Office Marketplace. Some offer trial versions so you can experiment with the service.

Trust Center

The Trust Center contains security and privacy settings for Office applications. To open the Trust Center and display the settings:

Hot tip

This shows opening the Trust Center from Word. It is similar for other Office applications, though the options offered may vary.

1 Select File, Options, and then select Trust Center

Don't forget

Click the links in the Trust Center to display information about Microsoft support, for privacy and security.

2 Click the Trust Center Settings button and choose an option, for example, Macro Settings, to see the details

Hot tip

Make changes, when required, to run macros that you create or that you receive from a reliable source, but restore settings to their original values when you've finished working with the associated document.

3 Select Add-ins to apply more stringent control over these

12 Where Next?

This provides a quick overview of other Office applications that may be in your edition, and shows you how you can use products that integrate with Office, or that share its formats. Finally, we look at using Office online, with Office Web Apps and SkyDrive folders.

Other Office Applications

We have looked at the main Office applications (Word, Excel, PowerPoint, Outlook, and OneNote) and the Office Tools in some detail, and taken a quick preview of Access and Publisher. Depending on which edition of Office you have, there may be other applications included. The editions and applications include:

Don't forget

Editions of Office:
Office 2013 RT
RT   Home and Student
Office 2013
H&S   Home and Student
H&B   Home and Business
Std   Standard
Pro   Professional
Pro+   Professional Plus
Office 365
Home Home Premium
University
Bus   Small Business
Professional Plus
Enterprise
Office 2013 Web:
Web   Office Web Apps

Windows RT 8.1 includes Outlook 2013 in addition to the four applications that were included in Windows RT 8.0.

Office 2013 RT	RT8	RT8.1			
Office 2013	H&S	H&B	Std	Pro	Pro+
Office 365				Home	Bus
Office 2013 Web	Web				
Word	Y	Y	Y	Y	Y
Excel	Y	Y	Y	Y	Y
PowerPoint	Y	Y	Y	Y	Y
OneNote	Y	Y	Y	Y	Y
Outlook	–	Y	Y	Y	Y
Publisher	–	–	Y	Y	Y
Access	–	–	–	Y	Y
InfoPath	–	–	–	–	Y
Lync	–	–	–	–	Y
Project	–	–	–	–	–
Visio	–	–	–	–	–

Systems with Microsoft Office 2013 Professional Plus or with one of the Office 365 business editions offer the most complete set of applications, as this Start screen illustrates:

Don't forget

All the applications are also available in stand-alone editions. For the Project and Visio applications, this is the only way to obtain them.

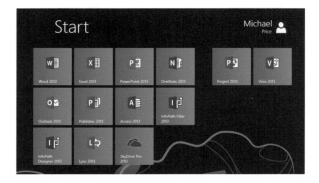

This also shows the two applications that are stand-alone only.

Office 2013 and Office 365

The major difference between these two Office suites is the pricing and licensing mechanisms.

Office 2013 editions are purchased for a one-time fee, and no more payment is required until you update to a new version. The purchase entitles you to use the software on one computer only.

Office 365 uses a subscription method, so you pay a yearly charge based on the edition you choose. This entitles you to use the software on up to five computers, and you can apply upgrades whenever they become available.

Both suites contain selections from the same set of applications, though as the table opposite shows, the Office 365 editions all include more products than the Home editions of Office 2013.

The Office 365 suite is usually the best choice for larger businesses and corporations. The Office suite that is most suitable for home or smaller business use depends on how many licenses you need, how often you expect to upgrade the applications and which specific applications and services you require.

To compare the suites:

1 Go to **office.microsoft.com** and select Products

2 Select the Compare link for Home or for Business

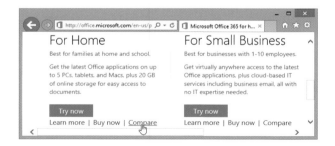

Hot tip

If your system is always connected via Wi-Fi or via the mobile network, you can also consider a fully online solution using the Office Web Apps (see page 230) if these offer enough function to meet your needs.

221

Don't forget

The Office editions for the larger businesses and enterprises are available on a per user basis and offer advanced corporate services.

...cont'd

Don't forget

The prices vary according to your region. In these examples the prices are for the United States.

Hot tip

Example scenarios:

2 PCs, 5 years between upgrades, basic products:
Office 365 HP $500
Office 2013 H&S $280

4 PCs, 5 years between upgrades, basic products:
Office 365 HP $500
Office 2013 H&S $560

1 PC, 5 years between upgrades, full products:
Office 365 HP $500
Office 2013 Pro $400

2 PCs, 5 years between upgrades, full products:
Office 365 HP $500
Office 2013 Pro $800

1 PC, 3 years between upgrades, full products:
Office 365 HP $300
Office 2013 Pro $400

(Prices correct at the time of printing.)

3 Locate and select the link to Compare Office suites

> Buy Office for Business ⊕
>
> Compare Office suites
> Common questions
> Free Office trial
> System requirements

4 Review the charges and features for the editions of Office displayed, in this case Office 365 Home Premium, and Office 2013 Home & Student, Home & Business and Professional

	Office 365 Home Premium	Office Home & Student 2013	Office Home & Business 2013	Office Professional 2013
	Office for your whole household	Managing home and homework just got easier	The freedom to do it all, virtually anywhere work happens	Best in class tools to grow your business
Student, teacher or faculty staff? See if you qualify for educational pricing.	$99.99 per year / Buy now / Try now	$139.99 / Buy now	$219.99 / Buy now	$399.99 / Buy now
Number of installations:	5 PCs or Macs plus up to 5 mobile devices	1 PC	1 PC	1 PC
Licensed for:	Home use	Home use	Home or business use	Home or business use
Core Office applications: Word, Excel, PowerPoint, OneNote	●	●	●	●
Email, calendars, and tasks: Outlook	●		●	●
Publishing & databases: Publisher , Access	●			●
SkyDrive® +20GB storage: Save documents online to your SkyDrive for easy access and sharing virtually anywhere	●			
Skype world minutes: Find new ways to stay in touch with 60 minutes of Skype calls each month to phones in 40+ countries	●			

5 Decide on your requirements and identify your options and their relative costs

As the example scenarios indicate, if you need more than a couple of licenses, or require the fuller function editions or want to upgrade more often than every five years, you are very likely to find Office 365 Home Premium the best choice for home use.

InfoPath Designer and Filler

InfoPath is used to design, view and fill out electronic data entry forms, in XML format. It is split into two applications, InfoPath Designer to create forms, and InfoPath Filler to complete them.

InfoPath provides controls, such as Textbox, Radio Button and Checkbox. There is also Repeating Table, and other repeating controls. For each of these controls, Rules can be defined to specify actions that will be performed under certain conditions.

 1 Select InfoPath Designer 2013 to select or create a template for the form you want completed

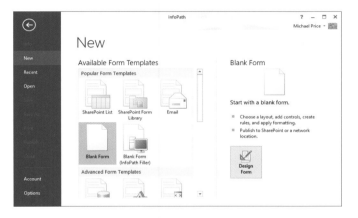

InfoPath will interoperate with a SharePoint Form Library so that forms can be completed offline and synchronized later. Forms can be embedded into web pages, or distributed and submitted through email. You can also create a form that can only be filled out using InfoPath Filler. To complete the form:

2 Select InfoPath Filler 2013 from the Start screen

3 Open the form that was created using InfoPath Design, complete the fields and save the form

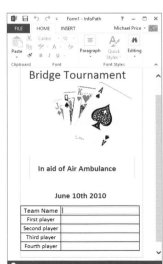

Hot tip

InfoPath forms can have fields pre-entered, entries can be validated as they are typed, and there can be links to information sources, to help fill out the details.

Don't forget

When the form has been designed, it must be published to shared storage, such as a web page, a workspace, a network drive or to a shared hard drive.

Beware

Using a form that can only be filled out using InfoPath Filler does, of course, mean that everyone who responds must have that product installed.

Lync 2013

Lync 2013 is available in the high-end Office 2013 Pro Plus and in the business editions of Office 365. With Lync you can have instant conversations, video conferences, online meetings, share files and work collaboratively.

For Lync to operate, your organization needs to install and set up Lync Server 2013. This requires a 64-bit operating system, since there is no 32-bit version. If you do not have Lync Server 2013, Microsoft offers a 180 day free trial to let you explore the options.

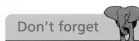

Don't forget

Like InfoPath 2013, Lync 2013 is designed for the larger business and is not intended for the home or small business user.

1 At **www.microsoft.com**, search for Lync 2013 free trial

Hot tip

Lync is also available as a Lync Mobile app for phones of all types and is accessible as a Lync Web App, so you can join a Lync meeting even if you don't have Lync 2013.

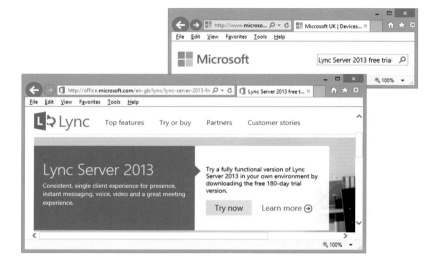

2 Download and install the trial to experiment with Lync

For home and small business use, you can achieve similar benefits using the Skype app which is available from the Windows Store

Hot tip

Skype allows users to communicate with peers by voice using a microphone, video by using a webcam, and instant messaging over the Internet. You can also make phone calls.

SkyDrive and SkyDrive Pro

Office 2013 can use your SkyDrive (see page 16). This is online storage associated with your Microsoft account and managed on your behalf by Microsoft at **www.skydrive.com**. SkyDrive is available to any user who registers a Microsoft account, and the service offers up to 7 GB of free storage. Additional storage is available for an annual charge. With SkyDrive you can work with your data files from any computer with Office 2013 or via the Web browser using the Office Web Apps (see page 230).

There are apps available to allow you to access your SkyDrive files

Don't forget

The price varies according to your region. In the United States, the annual charge is $10 for 20 GB of additional storage. (*Prices correct at the time of printing.*)

using your mobile phone. There are also Windows apps available to manage local copies of your SkyDrive files and folders, so that you can continue to work even when offline, knowing that the documents will be automatically synced the next time you connect.

For business users, Microsoft provides the SkyDrive Pro app. This supports storage that is hosted and managed by your business organization, using SharePoint Server software. The storage may also be hosted on the Internet, using SharePoint Online services.

You can store and organize your work documents or other files in your personal SkyDrive Pro library, and from there you can share files and collaborate on documents with co-workers in your organization. If you are signed in to Office 365, you may also be able to share documents with partners outside of your organization.

Hot tip

With SharePoint Online, each user will have 7 GB of personal storage capacity allocated to them. For on-premises SharePoint 2013 setups, the per-user storage capacity is a configurable parameter that the site administrators will manage.

Stand-alone Applications

There are some applications that are part of Microsoft Office 2013, but are not included in any of the Office editions.

Project

This is a specialized product that provides all the software tools and functions you require to manage and control a project. It handles schedules and finances, helps keep project teams on target, and integrates with other Office applications.

Don't forget

The file extension for Project 2013 is .mpp, and it is also compatible with Project 2010. Project 2007 and Project 2000–2003 use the same extension, but are treated as separate file types.

There are two versions – Standard and Professional – which add enhanced resource management, collaboration tools and project-management capabilities (supported by Office Project Server).

Visio

This is drawing and diagramming software, to help you visualize and communicate complex information. It provides a wide range of templates, including business process flowcharts, network diagrams, workflow diagrams, database models, and software diagrams, and makes use of predefined SmartShapes symbols. There are sample diagrams, with data integrated to provide context, helping you decide which template suits your requirements.

Don't forget

Visio 2013 is available in two editions. Standard offers the basic set of diagramming tools. Professional adds real-time dynamic visuals. The Visio Premium found in previous versions is no longer offered.

MapPoint 2013

MapPoint applications can be integrated into Office 2013 applications. There are two main MapPoint products:

MapPoint North America 2013

Microsoft MapPoint software includes detailed geographic coverage for the United States, Canada, and Mexico (no address find). Mapping coverage outside of those regions is limited to political boundaries and populated places.

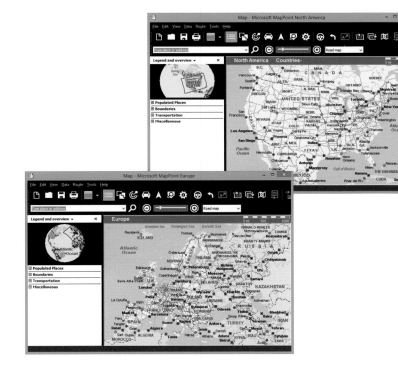

227

Don't forget

Some products can be integrated with Office 2013, even though they are not explicit components of Office.

Beware

You may have some items to install before you can install MapPoint itself.

Hot tip

There's a 14-day free trial of these products available as a download. See **www.microsoft. com/mappoint** for details of free trials.

MapPoint 2013 Europe

This provides detailed street-level mapping and address-find capability for Austria, Belgium, Denmark, Finland, France, Germany, Greece, Italy, Luxembourg, the Netherlands, Norway, Portugal, Spain, Sweden, Switzerland, and the United Kingdom.

In addition, MapPoint Europe provides some street-level coverage, but does not support address find, for Andorra, Bulgaria, Croatia, the Czech Republic, Estonia, Guernsey, Hungary, Ireland, the Isle of Man, Jersey, Latvia, Liechtenstein, Lithuania, Monaco, Poland, Romania, San Marino, Slovakia, Slovenia, and Vatican City.

Using MapPoint with Office

When you install MapPoint, add-ins are installed into Office applications, so you can use MapPoint 2013 to insert maps into Office documents and presentations directly from the application. For example, to insert a map into a Word 2013 document:

Don't forget

MapPoint is designed to work with Microsoft Office programs to create maps from data stored in an Office document or database and to insert maps into documents and presentation.

1 Open the document, select the Insert tab, then click the Object button in the Text group

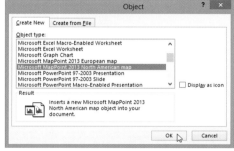

2 From Object, select MapPoint 2013 Map and click OK

3 The selected version of MapPoint will open

4 Locate the map section required for the document, using the MapPoint 2013 menus and toolbar

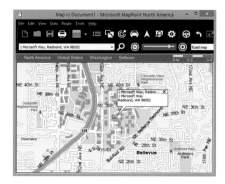

5 Select File, Exit & Return to Document

Hot tip

Double-click the map to open MapPoint and make any required changes to the map.

5 The map is inserted in the document which can now be completed and saved

Working with Other Products

Applications that do not directly integrate with Microsoft Office will usually accept files in Office document formats, as input. For example, to place a Word document in Adobe InDesign CS6:

1 Start InDesign and open a document (new or existing)

2 Select File, Place

3 Navigate to a Word file you want to add

4 Select the file and click Open

Don't forget

The InDesign document will not necessarily have many paragraph styles defined, initially.

Hot tip

The InDesign document will inherit the paragraph styles used in the Word document.

5 To override Word styles, create styles in the InDesign document, using the same names as the Word styles, and these will be used when the Word document is placed

Office Web Apps

If you have a Microsoft Account and associated SkyDrive, you can use Office Web Apps to create or access your Office documents from a browser, and share files and collaborate with other users online. You don't even need a copy of Office on the machine that you are using.

To use Office Web Apps:

1 Open Internet Explorer and go to **www.skydrive.com** If you are signed in to your Microsoft account (as for example when using Windows 8) your SkyDrive appears

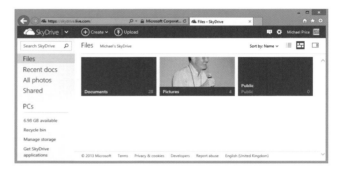

2 Open a folder and select an existing Word document

3 The document is opened in Reading view in the browser

Hot tip

If you aren't currently signed in to a Microsoft account, you'll be asked to sign in (or sign up for an account).

Don't forget

In SkyDrive, select Create and choose an Office Web App to create a Word, Excel, PowerPoint, or OneNote document in the current folder using the browser.

4 Click Edit Document and select Edit in Word Web App

5 The document is opened for editing in the browser

Hot tip

Select Edit Document, Edit in Word to open the document immediately in Microsoft Word.

6 The Word Web App has limited function, so to get the full capabilities select Open in Word

Don't forget

If you do not have Word 2013 installed on the computer, you'll get an error message.

7 If you select an Excel spreadsheet from SkyDrive, it will open for edit in the browser

Don't forget

You'll be warned if there are features that are not handled by the Office Web App version of the application.

My Office

Hot tip

My Office provides you with another way to access your documents and the Office Web Apps from your browser.

1 Go to the website **office.microsoft.com** and select My Office

2 You'll be prompted to sign in to Office.com using your Microsoft Account (or Corporate account for Office 365)

Don't forget

Your Recent documents are displayed, along with a link to your SkyDrive.

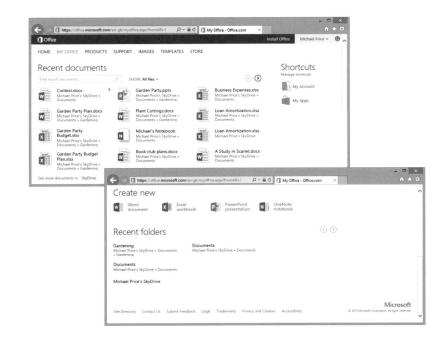

Don't forget

Scroll down and you'll see shortcuts to create documents using any of the four Office Web Apps, along with links to Recent folders.

G

H

I

J

K

L

P

Q

X

Y

Z

THE HENLEY COLLEGE LIBRARY